# everything
# is bad for
# you

# everything
## is **bad** for
## you

*An A-Z Guide to What You Never Knew Could Kill You*

## david french

SOURCEBOOKS HYSTERIA™
AN IMPRINT OF SOURCEBOOKS, INC.®
NAPERVILLE, ILLINOIS

This publication is sold with the understanding that the publisher is not
engaged in rendering legal, accounting, or other professional service. If
legal advice or other expert assistance is required, the services of a com-
petent professional person should be sought.—*From a Declaration of
Principles Jointly Adopted by a Committee of the American Bar
Association and a Committee of Publishers and Associations*

Published by Sourcebooks, Inc.
P.O. Box 4410, Naperville, Illinois  60567-4410
(630) 961-3900
FAX: (630) 961-2168
www.sourcebooks.com

Hardcover edition cataloged as follows:

French, David S.
  Everything is bad for you! : An A–Z Guide to What You Never Knew
Could Kill You / by David French.
      p. cm.
  1. Anecdotes. 2.  Conduct of life—Anecdotes. 3.  Wit and humor. I. Title.
  PN6261 .F68 2005
  818'.5402—dc21

                                                           2002008131

Printed and bound in Canada
WC   10  9  8  7  6  5  4  3  2  1

With love and gratitude to Tana, who would like you all to know that she came up with the funny bits, and Alex, who provided the (very) odd reference to bad things even I didn't know about.

# introduction

Everybody knows that whatever you really crave is illegal, immoral, fattening, or otherwise bad for you. Cigarettes kill you, tanning gives you cancer, drinking leads to violence, sports utility vehicles foul the air and raise the highway death rate, and don't even think about sex. What nobody has told you until now, though, is that *everything* is bad for you: food, vitamins, Philadelphia, optimism, air conditioning, rain, being a man, being a woman, breathing.

This is especially true of the things you thought were best for you. Jogging wrecks your knees. Stopping smoking can leave you depressed, and so can holidays. Cleanliness makes you sick. Good health gives you asthma. Gardening may lead to cognitive dysfunction. Alfalfa sprouts can poison you.

In deciding how to react, you're damned if you do and damned if you don't. Eating red meat can give you cancer; becoming a vegetarian can make you lose sexual function. Having a cat gives your children asthma; not having a cat gives your children asthma. (I know, I know, but I've got the references to prove it.) Being alone raises your death rate; being with a partner leads to quarrels that depress your immune system; keeping pets exposes you to diseases and bites.

Even when the right amount of something is actually good for you, you're in constant danger of straying off the narrow path. Too much cholesterol doubles death rates, and so does too little. Too little vitamin E can lead to strokes, and so can too much. Working long hours gives you heart attacks, and so does working short hours. To fine-tune these things would require your constant, anxious attention.

How do you deal with such a scary world? You could take antidepressants, but they can give you photosensitivity reactions, interfere with prescription medicines, or raise your risk of contracting non-Hodgkin's lymphoma. Maybe all you can do is stay in bed with the covers over your head—except that bed rest is bad for you, and the covers are infested with dust mites.

I'm sorry I brought this up.

# everything
## is bad for
## you

## ACETAMINOPHEN (see also ASPIRIN)

When you wake up with a life-threatening hangover, maybe a big bottle of painkillers washed down with a Bloody Mary isn't the best solution. Taking too much acetaminophen, especially in combination with alcohol, has been linked to liver and kidney damage.

## AIR (see also BUSES, CARS, CITIES, POWER PLANTS, SMOG, SPORTS UTILITY VEHICLES, TRUCKS)

Let's hear it for affluence, everybody—thanks to the pollution that cars and industries generate, this entry could be about *you!* Sixty-two million Americans live in areas whose air contains such high levels of major pollutants that it's officially defined as unhealthy. Unhealthy air can cause preterm births, birth defects, brain and nerve damage, heart attacks, and long-term injury to the lungs. It's generally correlated with both mortality and hospitalizations, especially among the elderly. And if you think you can solve the problem by retreating to your air-conditioned office, read on.

## AIR CONDITONING

Next time it's a hundred degrees outside and you're sitting smugly in your nice, cool office, keep this in mind: pollution in an air-conditioned room is likely to be two to five times as great as in the air outdoors.

## AIRPLANE CABIN CREW, BEING (see also WORK)

One cabin-crew member in ten has been injured in flight, through collisions with drink trolleys, burns from galley equipment, slipping on walkways, or exposure to infected blood during in-flight emergencies. Flight crews may also be exposed to fumes from engine lubricants containing organophosphates, possibly causing irreversible health problems such as nervous system disorders—which could make that little demonstration with the oxygen masks a lot more complicated.

## AIRPLANE TRAVEL (see also CARRY-ON AIRLINE BAGGAGE, TRAVEL)

**Airplane**

Welcome to Air Agony! Here's what's on our in-flight menu for today: obstructed eustachian tubes, barosinusitis, facial pain, ankle edema, airsickness, deep vein thrombosis leading to pulmonary embolus, dehydration…Traveling by air can give you all these—not to mention the diseases you can catch from other passengers. If you wear contact lenses, air travel can irritate your corneas. It can also disrupt your body's circadian rhythms, cause frequent filling of evacuation bags in people with colostomies, and accentuate psychotic or other unpredictable psychological tendencies—so you might want to keep a sharp eye on that guy sitting next to you conversing with his bread roll. If you're a frequent flyer, you're running the risk of inhaling dangerous levels of organophosphates; you're also being exposed to cosmic radiation at a greater intensity than you'd experience at ground level. Thank you for flying with us, and please come again soon!

## AIRPLANES

If you're a nature lover, take the bus. Airplanes produce more greenhouse gases per passenger-mile than other forms of transport.

## AIRPORTS

If you live anywhere near an airport, you already know about the traffic, the jet noise (which by itself can double your risk of high blood pressure), and the bad vibrations from the crowds outside the lost luggage department. But you might not know you can get malaria from mosquitoes that hitch rides on planes coming from infected areas and then fly to your house and bite you.

## ALBUQUERQUE (see also CITIES)

Albuquerque's drinking water contains more arsenic—which can cause cancer of the liver, bladder, lungs, kidney, and prostate—than does the water of any other major American city. Albuquerque can also be deadly when encountered in spelling bees.

## ALFALFA SPROUTS (see also FOOD)

Have some health food! Alfalfa sprouts, the most common type of sprout in salad bars and produce departments, have been linked to a number of disease outbreaks due to contamination by salmonella and E. coli. In California between 1996 and 1998, more widespread outbreaks of food poisoning were caused by alfalfa sprouts than by anything else. However, this could be linked to the fact that in California between 1996 and 1998, people ate more alfalfa sprouts than anything else.

## ALL-TERRAIN VEHICLES (see also CARS, OFF-ROAD VEHICLES, TRUCKS)

Between 1985 and 1998, 3,825 people were killed and more than 950,000 were treated in emergency rooms in the U.S. as a result of ATV-related injuries. (And, although it didn't make the news, Bambi and Thumper are now off-roadkill.)

## ALLERGY MEDICINES (see also ANTIHISTAMINES, OVER-THE-COUNTER DRUGS)

The antihistamines in many allergy medicines may affect your ability to drive more than alcohol does. On the other hand, how well do you drive while you're sneezing?

## AMERICA (see also CHINA, DOMINICAN REPUBLIC, EGYPT, INDIA, KENYA, MEXICO, PERU, TUNISIA)

The U.S. has only 4 percent of the world's population, but it's responsible for 24 percent of the greenhouse gas emissions that are expected to cause increased disease, death, and economic disruption throughout the world. (See GLOBAL WARMING for more detail.) All together now: Oh, beautiful for smoggy skies...

## AMERICAN, BEING

There's nothing remotely funny about this, but being an American is a mixed blessing. In the decade *before* the events of September 2001, 36 percent of all terrorist attacks worldwide were directed at American interests. It is especially dangerous to be an American abroad. At any given moment, the U.S. State Department has a list of twenty or more countries Americans should avoid, and others they should think twice about visiting. In periodic "Worldwide Cautions" (for example, during tensions in the Middle East in October 2000, and following the atrocities in September 2001), the State Department warns of periods of heightened threat to American citizens and interests everywhere in the world.

## AMERICAN STUDENT, BEING AN

In a study of fifteen-year-olds in thirty-one countries, American students ranked fourteenth in science, fifteenth in literacy, and nineteenth in mathematics. But they came first in TV trivia, joystick skills, and marshmallow fluff consumption.

## AMUSEMENT RIDES

More than ten thousand people require emergency room treatment in the U.S. each year, and an average of four of these die, as a result of injuries sustained on rides at amusement parks and fairs. Not much amusement there.

## ANGER (see also MOODS)

Don't let this get you mad: if you're prone to anger, even if you have normal blood pressure, you're at significantly greater risk of having a heart attack or dying suddenly from heart disease.

## ANIMALS (see BATS, BIRDS, CATS, COWS, DOGS, DUCKLINGS, MICE, PETS)

## ANTIBIOTICS (see also PRESCRIPTION DRUGS)

Next time they ask if you're allergic to penicillin, you might want to say yes—for all our sakes. Overuse and misuse of antibiotics have led to the evolution of "superbugs," potentially deadly bacteria that are becoming next to impossible to treat, as well as bacteria that cause food poisoning and drug-resistant strains of diseases such as tuberculosis and gonorrhea.

## ANTIDEPRESSANTS, NOT TAKING

People who don't take antidepressants (in the form of selective serotonin reuptake inhibitors) are more likely to have heart attacks. Before you reach for the Prozac, though, keep reading.

## ANTIDEPRESSANTS, TAKING (see also PRESCRIPTION DRUGS, ST. JOHN'S WORT)

Antidepressants can give you photosensitivity reactions, including hives, rashes, or other skin eruptions. People have been known to become suicidal or violent after taking serotonin reuptake inhibitors. One study found a possible relationship between using tricyclic antidepressants and contracting non-Hodgkin's lymphoma. And recently there have been claims that certain antidepressants are addictive. If you're taking enough antidepressants, though, all this may not bother you too much.

## ANTIHISTAMINES (see also ALLERGY MEDICINES)

If you're old and it's winter, you're damned if you do and damned if you don't: colds and flu can be deadly, but the antihistamines in cold and flu medications (as well as indigestion tablets and sleeping pills) can give you side effects such as confusion, memory loss, disorientation, and blurred vision, which can lead to misdiagnosis and treatment for senility.

## ANTIQUE STORES (see also WORKPLACES)

Antique stores have high concentrations of molds, which can cause nasal stuffiness, eye irritation, and wheezing. If you're exposed to them for too long, you could end up with more severe reactions such as fever, shortness of breath, or mold infections in the lungs. (And that's just in America, where an "antique" is anything made before 1945. European antique stores can probably kill at ten paces.)

## ANXIETY (see also MOODS)

If you worry, you should worry. Anxiety (which, as the most common mental disability in the country, affects about twenty-three million Americans) can double your risk of asthma, arthritis, headaches, ulcers, and heart disease, as well as making middle-aged men more likely to die of strokes. Maybe you should put this book down now.

## APPLIANCES

In 1997, the most recent year for which data are available, seventy-six people died in the U.S. after being electrocuted by appliances such as television sets, battery chargers, fans, pumps, refrigerators, and air conditioners. The magnetic fields produced by appliances such as hair dryers, electric shavers, and vacuum cleaners may also increase the risk of miscarriages. Be safe—become Amish.

## ARKANSAS (and see STATES)

Arkansas is the fifth most unhealthy state in the U.S. Yes, of course we're going to tell you which states rank first through fourth.

## ARMPITS (and see BODY)

If you were thinking about smelling a young man's armpits this weekend, change your plans: it can have a depressive effect.

---

### ARTIST, BEING AN
#### (see also WORK)

"Suffering for your art" isn't just a cliché. Artists are at risk for repetitive motion conditions, respiratory and neurological disorders due to poor ventilation and toxic substances, dermatitis and other skin conditions from contact with irritating materials, and acute eye injuries from welding and woodworking.

---

## ASPIRIN, TAKING (see also ACETAMINOPHEN, OVER-THE-COUNTER DRUGS)

If this book is giving you a headache, think twice before you do anything about it. Long-term use of aspirin can cause bleeding and start you on the road towards ulcers. Aspirin may also have bad effects on pregnancy, especially if taken during the last trimester. Taking aspirin when you have the flu has been linked to Reye's syndrome, especially in children, possibly leading to swelling of the brain and liver failure. It also can bring on asthma attacks.

## ASPIRIN, NOT TAKING

Not taking aspirin, on the other hand, may increase your risk of suffering or dying from heart disease, strokes, prostate cancer, ovarian cancer, and pre-eclampsia during pregnancy (although probably not all at once). Maybe you should do something about that headache after all.

### ASTHMA (see also DISEASES)
You already knew that asthma attacks can't be good for you, but there's more (gasp!): being asthmatic increases your risk of heart disease by 33 percent.

## ATHEISM
Time to make your mom happy and start going to church again. If you are African American, not practicing a religion can increase your blood pressure.

### ATHLETE, BEING AN (see also SPORTS)
Athletes suffer from an unusually high rate of benign orgasmic headaches, otherwise known as headaches after sex. But if you're an athlete, you've got other things to worry about: nobody who reads this book is going to sleep with you anyway (see ATHLETE, BEING AROUND AN).

## ATHLETE, BEING AROUND AN
Turns out jocks aren't as sexy as you thought. Male athletes are six times more likely than other men to commit sexual assaults, and ten times more likely to commit acts of domestic violence.

## ATHLETE, FEMALE, BEING A
Women who play sports such as basketball, soccer, and volleyball are two to eight times more likely than men to tear their anterior cruciate ligaments. On the other hand, they appear to be two to eight times less likely to get into shouting matches with the referee.

### ATLANTA (see also CITIES)
Here's the city where you could find the world's largest painting (if you wanted to): "The Battle of Atlanta." Unfortunately, the battle of Atlanta isn't just a matter of history. Over a ten-year period, Atlanta had the sixth highest murder rate in the U.S., almost

two-and-a-half times the average for major American cities. Four Atlanta colleges are among the five riskiest in America, in terms of crime in the neighborhoods around their campuses. And Atlanta ranks fifth in the U.S. in terms of people dying due to pollution from power plants.

### AUTUMN (see also WINTER, SPRING, SUMMER)
Never mind all that pretty fall foliage: suicides increase when summer turns to autumn, and people born in autumn have a higher risk of Alzheimer's disease. Plus, early autumn is the height of the hurricane season.

## BABIES, HIGH BIRTHWEIGHT IN
Size does matter. Heavier babies are more likely to develop diabetes.

## BABIES, LOW BIRTHWEIGHT IN (see also
### CHILDBIRTH, PREMATURE)
Babies who are underweight at birth are more prone to develop high blood pressure in later life. They also do less well in school and are more likely to work at lower-paying, blue-collar jobs. Men who were small babies are less likely to marry. But hey—at least they won't have diabetes.

## BABY BOOMER, BEING A
Spare a thought for aging baby boomers still valiantly trying to stay as active as they used to be: they account for a sharp increase in sports injuries.

## BABY BOTTLES (see also BABY CARE, BOTTLE-FEEDING)
According to the environmental group WWF, baby bottles that have been bottle-brushed, dishwashed, or sterilized can release a chemical that may cause babies to suffer later in life from

reduced sperm production, increased prostate weight, or conditions such as endometriosis. As you'll find out, though, the answer isn't BREAST-FEEDING.

## BABY CARE (see BABY BOTTLES, BOTTLE-FEEDING, BREAST-FEEDING, CRIBS, DIAPERS, HIGH CHAIRS, INFANT CARRIERS, PACIFIERS, STROLLERS, TOYS, WALKERS)

## BALDNESS (see HEADS, BALD)

## BALLET DANCING (see also DANCING)

Professional ballet dancers get hurt as often, and suffer just as many serious injuries, as athletes in contact sports. Unfortunately, this will not convince your ballet-dancing son's eighth-grade classmates that he's as macho as the football players.

## BALLOONS

We all know kids' parties can drive you right out of your tree, but there are also more concrete risks involved. Some people may experience rashes, asthmatic attacks, or other allergic reactions to the latex of which many balloons are made.

## BALTIMORE (see also CITIES)

You know how in *Homicide: Life on the Street*, there are dozens of murders every week? That isn't fiction. Over a ten-year period, Baltimore's homicide rate ranked in the top ten of major American cities, almost double the average rate for major cities.

## BARBER, BEING A (see also WORK)

Barbers have an unusually high risk of dying from pulmonary tuberculosis. And we thought their major problem was likely to be brain death from hearing "So how 'bout them Dodgers/Jets/Bulls?" fifty times a day.

## BASEBALL (see also SPORTS)

Forget about Little League and those chummy Saturday games with the guys: baseball is the third most dangerous summer sport. Baseball players may also run a high risk of skin cancers because they spend so much time in the sun.

## BASKETBALL (see also SPORTS)

And don't go shooting hoops, either. Basketball heads the list of recreational activities with the most injuries.

## BATS (see also ANIMALS)

Time to stop worrying about bats getting in your hair: we've found something better for you to be nervous about. Fruit bats can carry the Nipah virus, which has no cure and is so deadly that the Centers for Disease Control and Prevention include it in the same class of viruses as Ebola and AIDS.

## BEACH ITEMS, INFLATABLE (and see BEACHES, HOLIDAYS)

Inflatable water wings, beach balls, and air mattresses have been found to contain tributyl and dibutyl tin, which can harm the immune and hormonal systems. Have a nice holiday.

## BEACHES (and see BEACH ITEMS, HOLIDAYS)

And nominated for the Elvis Award for the Least Dignified Way to Die: people who dig deep holes in the sand at beaches have been smothered when the walls of the holes collapsed on them.

## BEDDING (see also DUST)

Instead of counting sheep at night, maybe you should count dust mites: in forty-four million American homes, the sheets, pillows, and blankets hold enough allergens from dust mites to cause allergies, and in twenty-two million homes, they hold enough to cause asthma attacks. Sleep tight.

## BED REST
If you're reading this during an extended stay in bed, the best plan might be to stay there. People recovering from bed rest can suffer from fainting spells, and can take several weeks to readjust to a standing position.

## BETA-BLOCKERS (see also PRESCRIPTION DRUGS)
Beta-blockers are among more than three hundred prescribed medicines that have been associated with a wide range of lung problems. They can also lead to fatigue, bradycardia, hypotension, dizziness, and diarrhea. How badly does your beta need blocking?

## BICYCLE HELMETS (see also BICYCLES)
It looks like your mom was wrong when she said you should always wear your helmet. As more and more people have started using bicycle helmets, the rate of head injuries suffered by bicyclists has gone up by more than 50 percent, possibly because cyclists feel better protected and therefore take more risks.

## BICYCLES (see also BICYCLE HELMETS, BUSES, CARS)
In 1999, bicycle accidents in the U.S. caused almost one-and-a-half million injuries that required medical attention. In 1997, 813 bicyclists were killed in crashes with motor vehicles. Bicyclists can also develop tendon and knee problems, and are more likely to suffer from erectile dysfunction or impotence. Male cyclists: care to go for a jog today instead?

## BIOTECHNOLOGY (and see FOOD AID)
You'll be astonished to hear this, but genetic modification can

have unpleasant side effects. Pollen from corn genetically modified to produce its own pesticides can kill the caterpillars that produce monarch butterflies. Engineering sugar beets to resist herbicides allows heavier use of sprays that kill weeds, eliminating the skylarks that ate their seeds. Where weeds are cross-pollinated with engineered genes, they can become "super weeds" that resist herbicides themselves. Genetically altered food might also have harmful effects on nutrition, cause allergic reactions, make bacteria resistant to antibiotics, and be toxic. Do we really need square tomatoes that badly?

### BIRDS (and see ANIMALS)
Remember *The Birds*? Hitchcock may have been right: it looks like birds really are out to get you. More than 350 people have been killed as a result of kamikaze birds colliding with aircraft. Birds also carry diseases, including the West Nile virus.

Bird

### BIRDS, PET (see also ANIMALS, PETS)
And forget "Pretty Polly": pet birds can give humans psittacosis, which causes flu-like symptoms and can lead to severe pneumonia and other health problems.

## BLOOD TRANSFUSIONS
Here's one for the So-What's-the-Alternative? Department: massive blood transfusions can undermine the immune system.

## BODY, HAVING A (see ARMPITS, BROKEN BONES, EYES, FEET, HEADS [BALD, ROUND, and SMALL], LEGS [RESTLESS and SHORT], PAIN, RING FINGER, TEETH; see also FAT, SHORT, TALL, THIN)

## BODY IMAGES, MALE

A growing number of boys and men are obsessed with their bodies to the point of suffering from muscle dysmorphia, an excessive preoccupation with body size and muscularity, at the expense of their health, schoolwork, jobs, and personal relationships. In the worst cases, sufferers require hospitalization, become reluctant to leave the house, or attempt suicide. We blame Popeye and his biceps.

### BOSTON (and see CITIES, TRAFFIC)

Heading into town to watch the Red Sox lose to the Yankees again? Leave yourself plenty of spare time. In a survey of sixty-eight American cities, Boston was sixth worst in terms of traffic, with almost half of daily travel taking place in congested conditions.

### BOTTLE-FEEDING (see also BABY BOTTLES, BABY CARE, BREAST-FEEDING)

If you're bottle-feeding your baby, you may be more likely to get breast cancer than women who breast-feed for two years or more, and your baby has a higher risk of allergies, respiratory problems, ear infections, sudden infant death syndrome, diabetes, baby-bottle tooth decay, obesity, high blood pressure, and—in the developing world—malnourishment. He or she may also suffer intellectually. If you think you can get around the problems by nursing, however, see BREAST-FEEDING.

### BOWLING ALLEYS (see also WORKPLACES)

If you work in a bowling alley, you have an unusually high risk of dying from chronic obstructive pulmonary disease. The dangers of life in the fast lanes...

## BREAD (see also FOOD)

Sliced bread doesn't deserve its great reputation. If you're sensitive to gluten, eating bread can give you headaches or loss of coordination. Scientists from the U.S. and Australia have theorized that the refined starches in bread could increase insulin levels, which might make your eyeballs too long and lead to shortsightedness.

## BREAST-FEEDING (see also BABY CARE, BOTTLE-FEEDING)

If you breast-feed your baby for more than four months, he or she could have a greater risk of developing heart disease as an adult. Children with allergies who were breast-fed by mothers with asthma are at greater risk of developing asthma themselves. Since breast milk doesn't contain vitamin D, breast-fed children are more likely to develop rickets. And breast-feeding has been linked to an increased risk of babies developing atopic dermatitis. See BOTTLE-FEEDING; looks like the best solution is to stop feeding your baby altogether.

## BREAST IMPLANTS

If you have breast implants, you're more likely to get cancers of the brain and lung, and (at least if the implants involve silicone gel) may suffer from a range of problems including toxic shock syndrome, scarring, asymmetry, connective-tissue diseases from ruptured implants, and rheumatologic symptoms. Silicone gel implants can also interfere with the detection of breast cancer by obscuring mammography images of possible tumors. Maybe you should just buy a Wonderbra.

## BREATHING (see also AIR, DUST)

Stop breathing *now*. Breathing produces free radicals, which can prompt premature aging, wrinkles, hardened arteries, stiff joints, cataracts, and even cancer. You have been warned.

(We're not exactly sure how they did the studies to find this out. How did they find a control group?)

## BROKEN BONES, HAVING (and see BODY)

It looks like fractures are habit-forming: women who break bones between the ages of twenty and fifty are more likely to suffer broken bones after menopause.

## BROKEN BONES, NOT HAVING (and see BODY)

On the other hand, postmenopausal women who *haven't* had fractures are more likely to get breast and endometrial cancers. It's never too late to get into the habit—you could always get a helpful friend to start you off by breaking a couple of your fingers.

---

### BUSES

**(see also AIR, BICYCLES, CARS, CITIES, TRAFFIC, TRUCKS)**
Remember how we told you taking the bus was more environmentally sound than traveling by plane? We lied. Diesel fumes from buses contain more than forty substances considered to be hazardous air pollutants, contributing to asthma, lung cancer, and global warming. (And the fumes from the bus station toilets contain substances that can kill you even faster.)

---

## BYPASS SURGERY (see also MEDICAL PROCEDURES)

Of people who undergo heart bypass surgery, 2 to 5 percent suffer strokes, and more than 40 percent show a significant decline on tests of mental ability five years later. On the other hand, not having the surgery isn't going to improve your mental ability either.

## CALCIUM, NOT TAKING (see also MILK, NOT DRINKING)

Don't let your kids go without calcium! Children and teenagers who consume too little calcium may end up with osteoporosis later in life.

## CALCIUM, TAKING (see also MILK, DRINKING)

Don't let your kids take calcium! If they do, the lead that may be mined along with the calcium could give them lead poisoning, which can result in cardiovascular and kidney disease. The high levels of calcium taken by people undergoing kidney dialysis may lead to heart disease.

### CAMPING (and see HOLIDAYS)

No more happy campers. Campers in the Ohio and Mississippi River valleys and Southeastern states may be exposed to blastomycosis, a potentially fatal disease that can present as acute pneumonia or can affect the skin, bones, and genitourinary tract.

## CANCER CURES

So-What's-the-Alternative? Department (continued): children who survive cancer face six times the normal risk of getting new cancers in early adulthood as a result of the treatments that cured them. Men who are cured of testicular cancer by certain forms of chemotherapy have a heightened risk of heart and kidney problems later on (most men, however, have absolutely no problem with this trade-off). Long-term use of a drug widely used for treating breast cancer may cause cancer of the womb and increase the risk of deep vein thrombosis. Chemotherapy can have long-term negative effects on memory and the ability to concentrate. Of people whose cancers are cured by bone marrow transplants, 5 to 20 percent develop chronic kidney failure.

## CANDLES
Ditch those romantic candlelit dinners. Each year, candles are involved in an average of 6,800 home fires, resulting in ninety deaths and losses of $74 million.

## CAREGIVING
It's true: caring, altruistic people *do* get to heaven faster—whether they want to or not. If you're caring for a sick or disabled spouse, you're more likely to die than people not caring for a spouse. If you're caring for a family member with Alzheimer's, you could reactivate latent herpes infections or suffer from depression; and if your spouse dies from this condition, you can be left with decreased energy and enthusiasm for as long as three years. Caring for a schizophrenic can lead to catching colds or other infectious diseases.

## CARPENTER, BEING A (and see WORK)
Save a carpenter: buy plastic furniture. The dust produced while making furniture, cabinets, and other wood products can lead to cancer of the nasal cavities and sinuses.

## CARPET-LAYER, BEING A (and see WORK)
Save a carpet-layer: stick to wooden floors. Carpet-layers may suffer from a variety of knee symptoms and conditions, including bursitis or skin infections, as well as fluid buildup requiring aspiration.

## CARPETS (see also DUST)
The paranoiacs were right all along: your carpet *is* trying to kill you. Carpets are likely to contain dangerous levels of dust, including pesticides, carcinogens, and heavy metals such as lead, cadmium, and mercury.

## CARROTS (see also FOOD)

Having good night vision may not be worth it: smokers who eat carrots increase their chances of lung cancer.

## CARRY-ON AIRLINE BAGGAGE

And the next nominee for the Elvis Award for the Least Dignified Way to Die: 4,500 people are injured in the U.S. each year when carry-on luggage falls on them from overhead bins in airplanes.

## CARS (see also AIR, ALL-TERRAIN VEHICLES, BICYCLES, BUSES, GLOBAL WARMING, OFF-ROAD VEHICLES, SPORTS UTILITY VEHICLES, TRAFFIC, TRUCKS)

Now that all the smokers have been rounded up and locked in a big basement in Iowa, the Surgeon General has moved on—starting soon, every car in the country will come with a big warning sticker on the windshield. Here's your sneak preview: car exhaust contains chemicals that can give you heart attacks, anemia, immune system disorders, behavioral changes, impaired mental function, respiratory diseases such as asthma and bronchitis, and cancer; it also increases the rate of atopic sensitizations, allergic symptoms, and diseases in children. To give an idea of the size of the problem, about twenty thousand people die every year in Austria, France, and Switzerland alone because of traffic-related air pollution, which also causes more than 290,000 episodes of bronchitis in children and more than 500,000 asthma attacks in those countries each year. Cars are also a major source of carbon dioxide, the primary gas responsible for global warming. (Yes, the Surgeon General knows it's hard to drive with a sticker that size on your windshield. That's the *point*.)

## CARS, NEW

You know that great new-car smell? According to researchers in Australia, it actually consists of a range of chemicals including benzene, which is carcinogenic, and various other substances that, through prolonged exposure, can cause abnormalities in your unborn children. Mmm…benzene.

## CARS, OLD (see also AIR)

And that old-car smell isn't any better. Even in the U.S., older cars make the air dirtier; and in countries including Mexico, Nepal, India, Iran, and Egypt (to name only a few), old cars have been blamed for deadly levels of pollution, including lead in the air at concentrations up to three hundred times the maximum limit recommended by the World Health Organization.

## CATS, DARK-COLORED

Patients with allergic rhinitis who have dark-colored cats suffer more than those who have light-colored cats or no cats at all. If your evil mother-in-law has rhinitis, you know what to get her for her next birthday…

## CATS, HAVING (see also ANIMALS, PETS)

If you're having a baby, it's time to dump the cat. Pregnant women who clean cat boxes may be exposed to a parasite that can give their babies congenital toxoplasmosis, a condition that can require a lifetime of special care. Cats can also trigger asthma in children.

## CATS, NOT HAVING

Hang on—get the cat back! Children who aren't exposed to cats have an increased risk of asthma. (We know this completely contradicts the last entry, but that's research.)

## CELL PHONES

We know the world might collapse if you can't be reached, but we don't care: there are times when you need to turn off your cell phone. Seventy percent of cell phone calls are by people driving vehicles (probably because, what with today's TRAFFIC, people spend 70 percent of their time driving); and drivers using cell phones are four times as likely to have an accident, with the effect lasting as long as five minutes after a call has finished. According to the British Medical Association, "hands-free" car phones are as dangerous as hand-held phones. Cell phones can interfere with medical devices such as heart monitors and mechanical ventilators. They may also set off airplanes' warning systems and disrupt signals. False alarms can reduce pilots' confidence in their warning systems, as well as distract the crew, and cause fatal mistakes.

## CHARCOAL GRILLS

Those funny-looking hot dogs your brother-in-law always brings aren't the only danger at the family barbecue. In 1996, nineteen people in the U.S. died of poisoning by carbon monoxide from charcoal grills.

Grill

## CHEESES, SOFT (see also FOOD)

The spoonfuls of fat and thousands of calories may not be the only threat lurking in that Brie. The bacterium *Listeria monocytogenes* can contaminate soft cheeses (even if they're refrigerated), causing flu-like symptoms. When the bacterium infects pregnant women, it can lead to miscarriages or mental and physical damage to their fetuses.

## CHEMICAL MANUFACTURING WORKER, BEING A
### (and see WORK)

Chemical manufacturing workers exposed to lead age five years more quickly, in terms of later declines in memory and learning abilities. We bet your medical plan contains some very, very small print.

## CHEMOTHERAPY (see CANCER CURES)

## CHICAGO (and see CITIES, TRAFFIC)

Three of the country's twenty-five riskiest colleges, in terms of crime in campus neighborhoods, are in Chicago. Chicago ranks fourth in numbers of people dying due to pollution from power plants, and fourth in terms of the amount of daily road travel that takes place in congested conditions. Are you *sure* it's your kind of town?

## CHICKEN POX (see also DISEASES)

Not that anyone wants to get chicken pox anyway, but here's another good reason not to: people who get chicken pox may later develop shingles, an outbreak of a rash or blisters that can lead to blindness or to pain that can persist for years after the rash has healed.

## CHILD CARE (see also DAY CARE)

We wouldn't want to make you working parents feel guilty or anything, but children who spend most of their time in child care (whether with relatives and nannies or in preschool and day care centers) are three times as likely to have behavioral problems such as aggression, defiance, and disobedience compared with children cared for by their mothers. Or is that why you put them there in the first place?

## CHILDBIRTH, NIGHTTIME

One study found that babies born at night were twice as likely as babies born during the day to die in the first week of life. So why has nature decided that most babies should arrive at three in the morning?

# CHILDBIRTH, CAESAREAN

A caesarean section may sound like an attractive alternative to twenty hours of labor, but if you have one, you're nearly twice as likely to end up back in the hospital within two months due to problems such as surgical wound infections, uterine infections, or gallbladder disease.

# CHILDBIRTH, COMPLICATIONS IN

Even being born can be bad for you. Complications in childbirth, particularly those associated with hypoxia, significantly increase the odds of early-onset schizophrenia.

# CHILDBIRTH, PREMATURE (see also BABIES, LOW BIRTHWEIGHT IN)

Premature babies often have smaller brains, which are linked to lower IQs. Babies born even a few weeks prematurely are more likely to die in their first year from infections, breathing problems, birth defects, and sudden infant death syndrome. When they say, "Don't push yet," they're not kidding.

# CHILDHOOD GROWTH, FAST

If your next-door neighbor smirks because her toddler's twice the size of yours, show her this entry. Babies who become overweight in the first year of life may be more likely to suffer from diabetes later. Thinner babies whose growth accelerates rapidly after the age of one are more likely to have heart disease as adults.

# CHILDHOOD GROWTH, SLOW

But you'd better hope your kid overtakes hers in a few years. Children who grow relatively slowly between the ages of seven and fifteen are more likely to break their hips in their adult years.

## CHILDREN, NOT HAVING
All this may have put you off having babies, but don't make up your mind yet: women who don't have children are more likely to develop breast and ovarian cancer than women who do. On the other hand, they have the option of buying white sofas.

## CHILDREN, UNWANTED
Unwanted children are twice as likely to engage in criminal behavior as those who were wanted. Of *course* you were a planned pregnancy, sweetie.

## CHINA (see also AMERICA, DOMINICAN REPUBLIC, EGYPT, INDIA, KENYA, MEXICO, PERU, TUNISIA)
We've all dreamed of taking that around-the-world trip of a life-time, but by the end of this book, we promise you'll feel better about staying home—because have we got a world tour for you! First stop, the Great Wall of China, if you make it that far. Unless you're Chinese, China is bad for you. In a study of more than 31,000 tourists, almost 30 percent of those who traveled to China got sick. (And just wait till we get to the Dominican Republic.)

## CHINESE FOOD, COOKING (see also FOOD)
Even if you *are* Chinese, actually, China can be bad for you. An unusually high proportion of Chinese women suffer from respira-tory problems due to breathing fumes from cooking.

## CHINESE MEDICINES (see also GINKGO BILOBA, HERBAL REMEDIES)
And don't try going to a Chinese doctor for a cure: some tradi-tional Chinese medicines contain unsafe quantities of steroids, as well as mercury and arsenic compounds or other ingredients that can cause allergic reactions, convulsions, blindness, kidney failure, heart palpitations, or cancer.

## CHOCOLATE, EATING (see also FOOD)

Eating chocolate is bad for you (surprise, surprise): it's low in fiber and high in calories, fat, and sugar.

## CHOCOLATE, NOT EATING

WARNING: LETTING YOUR KIDS SEE THIS ENTRY MAY LEAD TO ENDLESS ARGUMENTS IN CHECKOUT LINES. Chocolate contains antioxidant flavonoids that may help protect arteries and prevent heart disease—so *not* eating it is bad for you. (If you're premenstrual, not eating chocolate can also be bad for anyone near you.)

## CHOLESTEROL, TOO LITTLE

Have a hamburger. The death rate doubles for people with too little cholesterol.

## CHOLESTEROL, TOO MUCH

Put that hamburger down. The death rate doubles for people with too much cholesterol.

## CHRISTMAS
### (and see HOLIDAYS)

A study in the U.K. found that nearly one person in three has negative feelings about Christmas, and more than one in five says Christmas is stressful or a source of anxiety. (The other four were found huddled behind their Christmas trees, rocking back and forth and whimpering "RUM-pa-pum-pum, RUM-pa-pum-pum...")

## CIGARETTES (see SMOKING)

## CIGARETTES, LOW-TAR (see also CIGARS, SMOKING)

After you put so much effort into switching to low-tar cigarettes, we've got some bad news for you: it may have done you more harm than good. You'll just take longer and deeper drags, possibly increasing your risk of lung adenocarcinomas.

## CIGARS (see also SMOKING)

A cigar isn't just a cigar: it's a health hazard (and a political hazard, too). Smoking cigars can give you oral, esophageal, laryngeal, and lung cancers (although those aren't the ones Monica should worry about), as well as coronary heart disease and chronic obstructive lung disease. A misplaced cigar can also come (no pun intended) pretty close to getting you impeached.

## CIRCUMCISED, BEING (see also MEDICAL PROCEDURES)

Circumcision can result in surgical complications, disfigure the penis, interfere with local blood circulation, disrupt the relationship between male babies and their mothers, and have bad effects on the brain's perception centers. Women enjoy sex less if their partners have been circumcised, and so do their partners. This may explain a lot of Woody Allen movies.

## CIRCUMCISED, NOT BEING

Don't cancel your son's bris just yet, though. Not being circumcised may increase his risk of contracting bladder infections, HIV, and penile cancer.

## CITIES (and see ALBUQUERQUE, ATLANTA, BALTIMORE, BOSTON, CHICAGO, COLUMBUS, DALLAS, DETROIT, FALLON, HOUSTON, LOS ANGELES, MIAMI, NEW ORLEANS, NEW YORK,

NORMAN, PHILADELPHIA, PHOENIX, PORTLAND, RICHMOND, SAN DIEGO, SAN FRANCISCO, SEATTLE, ST. LOUIS, WASHINGTON; see also AIR, RURAL AREAS, TRAFFIC)

Children living in cities are more likely to have asthma. If you're a city-dweller, you're almost twice as likely as someone living in a rural area to be a victim of a personal crime, and you're much more likely to be murdered: the seventy-seven largest U.S. cities are home to 20 percent of the U.S. population but account for 50 percent of all homicides. On the other hand, you have a greatly reduced risk of being arrested for cow-tipping.

## CLEANLINESS (and see DIRTINESS, SOAP)

Bad news for obsessive-compulsives: if you're living in a spick-and-span environment with no bacteria or viruses around, your immune system may become weak from lack of exercise, triggering illnesses including asthma, allergies, autoimmune diseases such as rheumatoid arthritis, and the most severe type of diabetes. The antibacterial agents in soaps, detergents, and sprays simply produce stronger bacteria that are resistant to these agents.

## COCAINE (see also DRINKING, ECSTASY, MARIJUANA)

Using cocaine can give you aneurysms in heart arteries, heart attacks, and strokes. It can also give you a police record and one-nostril syndrome.

## COFFEE, DRINKING (see also DRINKS, TEA)

Drinking coffee can make anxiety and panic disorders worse (which explains a lot about New York), and it's been shown to harm the aorta. It also increases your risk of miscarriages and of developing carpal tunnel syndrome. Drinking unfiltered coffee can increase cholesterol levels. Smokers who drink coffee increase their risk of lung cancer. How has our society survived this long?

## COFFEE, NOT DRINKING

People who don't drink coffee (all four of you) are more likely to contract Parkinson's disease and, especially if they smoke, cancer of the bladder.

### COINS (and see DOLLAR BILLS)

Coins

Believe it or not, the hard-hearted types who claim you're hurting the homeless by giving them your spare change may actually have a point: nickels, dimes, quarters, and half-dollar coins all contain nickel, which can cause skin reactions in people with a nickel allergy.

### COLLEAGUES (see also OFFICES, WORK)

Unsupportive colleagues at work can give you forearm pain. The studies didn't show whether this comes from punching them.

### COLUMBUS, OHIO (and see CITIES)

Columbus is the fifth fattest city in America. We have no idea how they figured this out.

### COMPUTER GAMES (see also MOVIES, TELEVISION, VIDEO GAMES)

Children who play computer games can end up with bad posture and repetitive strain injury, especially a form known as "Nintendo thumb," which sounds like a wrestling move but is actually even more painful.

### COMPUTERS (see also INFORMATION TECHNOLOGY, INTERNET)

Maybe you really *are* allergic to work. The plastic in computer casings can give off fumes that make you itch, block up your nose, and give you headaches. The repetitive hand movements involved in using a computer can leave you with carpal tunnel syndrome, whose symptoms include burning, tingling, or numbness of the fingers, as well as difficulty gripping tools and making a fist.

### CONDOMS (see also DIAPHRAGMS, PILL, SPERMICIDES)
Next time you use a condom, spare a thought for those who suffered so you could have safe sex: some workers in condom factories suffer from rhinoconjunctivitis and asthma caused by the powder in which condoms are packed. Condom users themselves may suffer rashes or more serious allergic or irritant reactions to the latex from which condoms are made. (That would be a pretty effective contraceptive, actually.)

### CONSERVATIVE, BEING
People with right-wing political views are more likely to have nightmares or dreams that feature aggression and violence. This is even more disturbing when you consider that these are probably the same people who own large numbers of guns.

### CONSTRUCTION WORKER, BEING A (and see WORK)
Do something nice for construction workers today: live in a tent. Construction workers have an unusually high risk of dying from pneumoconiosis, silicosis, and respiratory conditions due to chemical fumes and vapors. On the other hand, given the things they shout when you walk past construction sites, maybe you'd rather have them build you a five-story mansion.

### CONTRACEPTIVES
There's no such thing as safe sex. (See CONDOMS, DIAPHRAGMS, PILL, SPERMICIDES.)

### CORRECTION FLUID (and see OFFICE SUPPLIES)
After four or five years in accounts receivable, sniffing correction fluid might sound like a good idea. Wrong. Ninety-one office

workers in the U.K. were injured by correction fluid during the year 2000.

## COTTON CLOTHES, HOSPITAL VISITS IN
Here's one the Spanish Inquisition never thought of: death by T-shirt. Wearing cotton clothing in hospitals can transmit the Aspergillus fungus, which can cause fatal infections in patients with impaired immune systems.

### COWS (and see ANIMALS)
Every year, every grass-eating cow produces 120 kg of methane, a greenhouse gas twenty times more damaging than carbon dioxide. This can add up: in Ireland, for example, farting and belching by cows accounts for about 35 percent of total green-house gas emissions. We think this was discovered by a bunch of ecstatic twelve-year-old boys who figured they'd come up with the best science project *ever*.

## CREATINE
According to France's *Agence de Sécurité Sanitaire des Aliments*, creatine (used by many athletes as a training aid) causes digestive, muscular, and cardiovascular problems, and may pose long-term dangers to health. It could also increase the risk of cancer. And, to add insult to injury, it doesn't help much anyway.

### CRIBS (see also BABY CARE)
More than ten thousand children under the age of five were injured in 1999, and more than thirty die each year, as a result of crib injuries, including falls and suffocation. Most cribs inspected in a national sampling of motels and hotels were found to be unsafe. How could you think of anything funny to say about this?

## CRUSHING AND GRINDING MACHINE OPERA-TOR, BEING A (and see WORK)

Operating crushing and grinding machines is the occupation with the highest risk of dying from tuberculosis. If this makes you really mad at your employer, at least you have the perfect way of getting rid of him.

### DALLAS (and see CITIES)

Over a ten-year period, Dallas ranked in the top ten American cities in terms of its homicide rate, which was 1.8 times the average for major cities—and that's not even counting J.R.

### DANCING (and see BALLET DANCING)

Can you believe it? Putting all of your weight on the tips of your toes for long periods of time is actually *bad* for you. Professional dancers are at risk for acute injuries including stress fractures in the lower extremities, musculoskeletal problems, osteoporosis, amenorrhea from low body fat, and foot deformities including bunions, as well as performance anxiety and sleep disturbances.

### DATING

As if there weren't enough good reasons not to date high-school boys (acne, funny voices, lack of intelligible conversation), here's another one: 20 percent of high-school girls report being physically abused or forced into sexual activity by a dating partner. One-third of teenagers who date suffer psychological violence in their relationship. Boycott the prom!

### DAY CARE, NOT SENDING CHILDREN TO

OK, all you working parents can stop feeling guilty now. Children who aren't regularly exposed to other children—in day-care centers, for example—are more likely to develop asthma and frequent wheezing later in childhood.

## DAY CARE, SENDING CHILDREN TO (see also
### CHILD CARE)

Bring that guilt back. There's a relatively high incidence of sudden infant death syndrome in day-care settings, where caretakers may be less likely to know that it's important to put babies to sleep on their backs. Day-care centers also spread antibiotic-resistant bacteria that can cause infections of the respiratory system.

## DAY CARE, WORKING AT (and see WORK)

Yes, we all figured that working in a day-care center means you risk losing your mind. But it turns out that's not the only problem: it's the occupation associated with the highest risk of dying from asthma.

## DEATH PENALTY

If you live in a state that employs the death penalty, you're more likely to be a victim of homicide than if you live in a state without the death penalty. A case of citizens following the moral lead of their legislators?

## DEMENTIA

Think twice before you ask your neighbors to turn down the horrible music. Dementia can create an abrupt change in musical tastes, leading otherwise normal people to play pop music at loud volumes. You sure you want to go over there and yell at them?

## DENTIST, BEING A (and see WORK)

At least in the U.K., studies show that dentists have an unusually high suicide rate. (Of course, it's possible that some of these were accidents—the poor guy was doing his own filling and his hand slipped...)

## DEPRESSION (see also DISEASES)
If you're depressed, there's a good chance your condition will be misdiagnosed or wrongly treated. Properly diagnosed or not, depression can lead to or exacerbate heart disease and interferes with recovery from cancer, kidney failure, and hip fractures. It also makes middle-aged men more likely to die of strokes and weakens the immune system of older people. Are you sure you want to keep reading this book?

## DETROIT (and see CITIES)
Detroit is the second fattest city in America. It also had the second highest murder rate in the U.S. over a ten-year period—three times the average for major American cities. All the killers were acquitted, though: they used the Twinkie defense.

## DIAPERS
A study suggests that disposable diapers can raise the scrotal temperature of baby boys, which may (or may not) lead to infertility and testicular cancer in later life. Switch to cloth: your son would forgive you many things, but not that.

## DIAPHRAGMS
If you use a diaphragm, you're more likely to develop urinary tract infections than women who use other forms of birth control. That doesn't mean the other forms are good for you, of course: see CONDOMS, PILL, SPERMICIDES.

## DIETS
A high-protein diet with lots of red meat can give you heart disease. Low-carbohydrate diets may lead to ketosis, which can cause bad breath, nausea, and a nasty taste in the mouth. And low-fat diets can give you a whole variety of health problems. Looks like you should live on buttered toast (hey, it works for college students).

## DIOXINS (see also INCINERATORS)

People exposed to dioxins (which are produced by incinerators and were the active ingredient in Agent Orange, used to defoliate forests during the Vietnam War) are more likely to develop diabetes and various cancers, have damaged fertility, and produce fewer boy children. (This is only bad if you want a boy; if you want a girl, dioxin may help, but we still wouldn't recommend it.) And the problem takes a while to go away: thirty years after Agent Orange was last used in Vietnam, some villagers have as much as two hundred times the normal amount of dioxin in their bloodstreams.

---

### DIRTINESS

Good news for obsessive-compulsives: people with dirty hands have twice as much respiratory illness as people who wash their hands five times a day. Just don't think that the SOAP you're washing with is good for you.

---

## DISABLED, BEING

Compared with the rest of the population, the 54 million Americans with disabilities are less than half as likely to graduate from high school, only one-seventh as likely to own a home, and three times as likely to live in a household whose annual income is under $15,000. Not only that: even if all these problems could be solved, they'd still be disabled.

## DISASTERS, RECOVERING FROM (see also PEACE)

The only thing worse than being in a disaster is *having been* in one. After a natural disaster is over and people are recovering, they can develop anxiety disorders and other mental illnesses, and suicide rates increase.

**DISEASES** (see ASTHMA, CHICKEN POX, DEPRESSION, GUM DISEASE, INFLUENZA, RESPIRATORY INFECTIONS, SORE THROATS, VIRUSES)

## DISH CLOTHS

More proof that CLEANLINESS is bad for you: the cloths you use to dry dishes can serve as breeding grounds for the organisms that cause salmonella, campylobacter, and viral infections.

### DIVING (see also SPORTS)

Diving accidents cause 850 paralyzing spinal cord injuries each year, more than three hundred of which happen in home swimming pools. Stop trying to impress that sexy lifeguard—or your sexy neighbor.

### DIVORCE (see UNMARRIED, BEING)

## DO IT YOURSELF, TV PROGRAMS ON (see also GARDENING, TV PROGRAMS ON)

You know how fixing a roof or dealing with that leaky plumbing looks so easy on TV—right up until you try it yourself? You're not alone. TV programs explaining how to do household repairs make them seem simpler than they are. In the U.K., one study has shown a 27 percent rise in DIY accidents as people bite off more than they can fix.

## DOCTOR, BEING A (see also NURSE, WORK)

Doctors have unusually high rates of suicide (except the ones on daytime TV, who apparently live forever). They also suffer from work-related conditions such as contact allergic dermatitis, contracted by exposure to latex gloves or substances such as antimicrobials, formalin, and benzocaine.

## DOCTORS (see also HOSPITALS, MEDICAL DIAGNOSES, MEDICAL PROCEDURES, PRESCRIPTION DRUGS)

If you're not feeling well, the safest thing might be to take two pills and *not* call him in the morning. Medical errors kill nearly one hundred thousand Americans a year. It has been estimated that at any given moment, 3 to 5 percent of doctors are unfit to see patients, and the Public Citizen's Health Research Group has established a data bank of 20,125 doctors who have been disciplined for their mistakes.

## DOCTORS, MALE

Male doctors are more likely than their female counterparts to recommend mastectomy over lumpectomy for older women diagnosed with early-stage breast cancer, even where clinical indications for mastectomy are absent. Female doctors: don't think about this next time you have a patient with testicular cancer.

## DOCTORS' OFFICES, AFTERNOON VISITS TO

Next time you're going to the doctor, make sure you get up early. If you have undiagnosed diabetes, you're only half as likely to have it diagnosed if you visit your doctor in the afternoon instead of in the morning.

## DOCTORS' OFFICES, VISITS TO

Bring back house calls. Visiting a doctor's office may make it impossible to get an accurate blood pressure reading. Up to half of all readings may be either too high (because of the stress of being there) or too low (a condition termed "white coat normotension" that can disguise actual high blood pressure).

## DOGS (see also ANIMALS, PETS)

A dog is man's best friend—some of the time. In one recent year, 830,000 people required medical care in the U.S. as a result of dog bites. Over a two-year period, twenty-seven people—nineteen of them children—were killed by dogs. Sixteen of the twenty-seven were killed by rottweilers and pit bulls, breeds that accounted for two-thirds of people killed by dogs over the past twenty years. Barking dogs are a major problem: one study in the U.K. found dogs came second only to loud music among "emphatic noise complaints," and these problems account for serious friction between neighbors practically everywhere. Dogs also carry diseases such as leptospirosis and visceral canine leishmaniasis, which can be fatal to humans. Get a cat instead. (No, don't—see CATS.)

## DOG CHEWS

Dog chews can transmit salmonella infections—small children who come in close contact with dogs and their chews are especially vulnerable. But then, see DOGS; why would you want to give the mutt a treat, anyway?

### DOLLAR BILLS (and see COINS)

Bill Gates probably wouldn't agree, but money is bad for you. A study found that one dollar bill in fourteen was contaminated by microbes that could cause serious illness, while 90 percent carried germs, including the notorious "flesh-eating bug."

### DOMINICAN REPUBLIC (see also AMERICA, CHINA, EGYPT, INDIA, KENYA, MEXICO, PERU, TUNISIA)

And now, the next stop on our worrying world tour: the beautiful Dominican Republic! Most of us can't find it on a map, and maybe you shouldn't try: in that study of more than 31,000 tourists, 39 percent of those traveling to the Dominican Republic got sick.

## DOORBELLS

Jumping up to answer the doorbell can give you a stroke. (J.D. Salinger will live forever.)

## DOUBT, RELIGIOUS

If you're sick, don't let yourself start having doubts about God: He might not appreciate it. A study has found that older patients who doubt their faith while sick die sooner than those whose faith remains strong.

### DRINKING (see also HANGOVERS; and see COCAINE, ECSTASY, MARIJUANA)

Drinking

We all know that drinking can lead to embarrassing incidents involving putting someone's underwear on your head and serenading your girlfriend with a rendition of "Light My Fire," but that's only the tip of the iceberg. For young people, drinking can lead to violence (90 percent of all rapes on college campuses involve alcohol) or serious accidents (alcohol-related accidents are the leading cause of death among fifteen- to twenty-four-year-olds). Children born to drinking mothers can suffer from fetal alcohol syndrome, whose symptoms include low birthweight, distorted facial features, stunted growth, and mental retardation that may be irreversible. In a study of accidents in a wilderness area, alcohol played a significant role in one-half of all fatalities. Alcohol abusers are at particular risk of developing conditions such as carpal tunnel syndrome and hypertension. Even moderate drinking may make you more likely to suffer brain atrophy, which is associated with reduced neurological and cognitive function. Now put that traffic cone back where you got it.

## DRINKING, NOT

Great Excuse of the Day: if you don't drink, you're more likely to get diabetes, heart disease, and cancer (if it's red wine that you're not drinking) than people who do. Not drinking may also make you more likely than moderate drinkers to suffer white matter infarcts, which are associated with reduced neurological and cognitive function. Cut out this entry and take it with you to the bar. You still don't get to keep the traffic cone, though.

## DRINKS (see COFFEE, FRUIT JUICE, MILK, SOFT DRINKS, TEA, WATER; see also DRINKING, HANGOVERS)

## DRINKS, HOT (see also COFFEE, TEA)

Drinking hot beverages increases your risk of esophageal cancer. If you think reaching for something iced gets you off the hook, though, you're wrong; see DRINKING, SOFT DRINKS, etc. for the cold truth.

## DRY CLEANERS, WORKING IN (and see WORK, WORKPLACES)

Do something nice for your dry cleaner: hand-wash. Long-term exposure to dry-cleaning fluids can cause liver and kidney damage, memory loss, confusion, pneumonia, diseases of the stomach, and ischemic heart disease, as well as cancer of the tongue, bladder, esophagus, intestine, lung, and cervix.

## DUCKLINGS (see also ANIMALS, PETS)

Yeah, we know they're small and cute and fluffy, but it's always the harmless-looking ones. Handling ducklings and chicks has produced outbreaks of salmonellosis that are especially dangerous for children.

### DUST (see also CARPETS)

Dust consists partially of the waste from dust mites—found in significant numbers in nearly half of U.S. homes—which can give you allergic reactions such as headaches, sinus troubles, and loss of energy. Yet another reason why BREATHING is bad for you.

### EAST, THE (see also MIDWEST, SOUTH, WEST)

On America's east coast, increases in sea levels due to global warming are likely to cause substantial damage to structures, wetlands, estuaries, and water supplies. Warming will also increase urban heat stress, which is high on the list of things that do not need increasing. Major diseases new to the U.S., such as Lyme disease and West Nile virus, have started in the East.

### EATING TOO LITTLE (see also FOOD, THIN)

If you fell off your diet again, maybe you were doing yourself a favor. When women eat too little due to conditions such as anorexia nervosa, they may stop menstruating, become dehydrated, develop kidney stones and kidney failure, suffer from constipation or bowel irritation, develop osteoporosis, and grow hair on their faces and arms (which is why the women on most TV shows shave more than the men); in extreme cases, eating too little can make their muscles waste away and lead to irregular heartbeat, heart failure, and death. And if you're pregnant, go ahead and make yourself that tuna-and-jelly sandwich: if you have serious nutritional deficiencies during pregnancy, your child may end up suffering from diabetes, high blood pressure, and strokes, as well as conditions such as schizophrenia or affective disorders severe enough to require hospitalization.

### EATING TOO MUCH (see also FAT, FOOD)

But don't let that scare you into eating everything in the fridge.

Women who binge-eat risk polycystic ovary syndrome, which causes infertility.

### ECHINACEA (see also HERBAL REMEDIES)

Coming down with a cold? Before you reach for the echinacea, note that you can have allergic reactions to this, especially if you're allergic to plants to which echinacea is related, such as daisy and ragweed. Looks like you're going to end up with a drippy nose no matter what you do.

## ECONOMIC DEVELOPMENT, TOO LITTLE

Shock of the Week: being poor ain't good for you. In poor societies, inadequate shelter, diet, and security mean that people live in poor health, die early, and feel an overwhelming desperation about life that can take extreme forms such as sale or starvation of unwanted children, theft of body parts, and violent ethnic conflict.

## ECONOMIC DEVELOPMENT, TOO MUCH

The American Dream isn't all it's made out to be. In rich societies, people suffer from constant time pressures, too little sleep, feelings of anxiety and stress, and estrangement from family and community—any of this sound familiar? One study found that stress has increased so much in the U.S. that typical schoolchildren today may experience more anxiety than child psychiatric patients did during the 1950s. The risk of breast cancer and prostate cancer is greater in more affluent areas. Where development results in a shift from traditional diets to Western diets, there may be an increased risk of allergies and asthma. African Americans are more subject than Africans to dementia and Alzheimer's disease, probably because of dietary habits and other features of development. When Grandpa and Grandma get nostalgic about the Old Country, maybe they have a point.

## ECSTASY (see also COCAINE, DRINKING, MARIJUANA)

Using MDMA, commonly known as Ecstasy, can lead to psychiatric disorders or possible long-term impairments in brain function, to the extent that regular users frequently forget simple tasks and routinely lose their train of thought while talking, according to one study that...that...sorry, what was I saying? Risky sexual behavior among gay and bisexual men is also associated with Ecstasy—no, no, we mean the *drug*...

## EDUCATION, TOO LITTLE

The idea that college can have health benefits may not match your memories of your undergrad years, but it's true. People with less education are more likely to kill themselves, get Alzheimer's disease, and generally die early. If you don't have a college education, you'll recover less well, mentally, from coronary artery disease. People who live in communities with low education levels are more likely to be late in seeking treatment for melanomas, so their treatment is less likely to be successful.

## EDUCATION, TOO MUCH

But don't let that make you drag your six-week-old into an early learning program: putting pressure on kids to start formal education too soon can result in failure, long-term underachievement, disaffection, and truancy.

## EGGS (see also FOOD)

Of all the things people eat, eggs are second only to seafood as a cause of outbreaks of food poisoning, causing 660,000 illnesses and 330 deaths in the U.S. each year. And smokers who eat eggs increase their risk of lung cancer. (Why do we get the feeling that's going to make you give up omelets rather than cigarettes?)

## EGYPT (see also AMERICA, CHINA, DOMINICAN REPUBLIC, INDIA, KENYA, MEXICO, PERU, TUNISIA)

That trip of a lifetime has to include the pyramids, right? Wrong. In that same study of tourists, one-third of those who traveled to Egypt got sick.

## ELECTRICITY (see POWER LINES, POWER PLANTS)

---

### EL NIÑO

People have blamed El Niño for just about everything ("Our relationship just isn't working—it's not you, it's El Niño"), but it turns out to involve real dangers. The global weather patterns associated with El Niño have been linked to increases in illnesses such as malaria, cholera, dengue fever, and childhood diarrhea.

---

## EMBALMER, BEING AN (and see WORK)

We doubt that embalming is top of your career choice list, but if it is, please reconsider: embalmers have a greater risk of leukemia and brain cancer than the general population.

## EMERGENCY ROOMS (see also HOSPITALS, INTENSIVE CARE)

More than 90 percent of emergency room directors report over-crowding due to nationwide closings of hospitals and ERs, as well as difficulty in moving patients out of ERs into overcrowded intensive care units. This means it can be hard to find an ER willing to accept an emergency case, and once the case is accepted, there can be long waits for treatment. (There was a dip in the admission figures when Doug Ross left, but they went right back up again once Dr. Kovac arrived.)

## EMOTIONAL RESTRAINT (see also MOODS)

It's true, some situations call for a good cry: women who suppress their emotions following treatment for breast cancer experience more distress and have a less favorable health outlook. Or a good scream: women who try to suppress anger are likely to end up even angrier.

## ENERGY BARS (see also FOOD, HERBAL REMEDIES)

Energy bars may contain ingredients that could be harmful or even fatal, especially herbal ingredients such as ephedra, a stimulant that if misused can cause dangerously high blood pressure and a fast heart rate. Nobody needs an energy boost that badly, no matter how little you've studied for your chemistry final.

## EPHEDRA (see ENERGY BARS, WEIGHT-LOSS PRODUCTS; see also HERBAL REMEDIES)

## EPILEPSY DRUGS (see also PRESCRIPTION DRUGS)

So-What's-the-Alternative? Dept. (continued): the drugs women take to control epilepsy can make oral contraceptives less effective and increase the risk of birth defects.

### ERASERS (and see OFFICE SUPPLIES)

Eraser

The usual danger of erasers is that sooner or later your four-year-old will stuff one up his nose, but the consequences could be even nastier than you expect. People may experience rashes, asthmatic attacks, or other allergic reactions to the latex of which some erasers are made.

## ESTROGEN, NOT TAKING

You women know about your bones getting brittle if you don't take estrogen, but if you're post-menopausal with a hard-driving,

Type-A personality, not taking estrogen also increases your risk of heart problems. It's a bad combination: you could end up with a heart attack from breaking your hand while punching out your stupid boss.

### ESTROGEN, TAKING (see also HORMONE REPLACEMENT THERAPY, PRESCRIPTION DRUGS)

On the other hand, *taking* estrogen may increase your risk of uterine, breast, and ovarian cancer. Stay young.

## EXERCISE

Nowadays, there are only three things left that we believe in with total, unquestioning, evangelistic faith: exercise, sunscreen, and drinking eight glasses of water a day. So brace yourself: we're about to shatter one-third of the Holy Trinity. People who get lots of exercise are less likely to live into old age. If you somehow get as far as your fifties, lots of exercise may lead to memory loss or premature senility. (See also SUNSCREEN and WATER—if you think you can take it.)

## EXERCISE, ISOMETRIC

And if you think isometrics are the kinder, gentler way to fitness, think again. Isometric exercise produces sudden increases in blood pressure that can be risky, especially if you have cardiovascular weakness or disease.

## EXERCISE, NOT GETTING

All you couch potatoes can stop snickering now. Lack of exercise and obesity contribute to up to a third of cancers of the colon, breast, kidney, and digestive tract. Depressed people who don't exercise are more likely to have their depressions recur after treatment. Walking between the fridge and the remote control doesn't count.

## EYES, LIGHT-COLORED (see also BODY)
People with light-colored eyes may be more likely to get meningitis and to become deaf as a result. (How do people think up these studies? And how do they ever get funding?)

## EYESIGHT, NORMAL
And who thought of looking for *this?* Women with normal eyesight are twice as likely as blind women to develop breast cancer.

## FALL (see AUTUMN)

## FALLON, NEVADA (and see CITIES, NEVADA)
If you live in Fallon (which, fortunately, isn't likely), don't drink the water. Fallon's drinking water has one of the highest levels of arsenic contamination in America—ten times the limit recommended by the World Health Organization—and arsenic can cause cancer of the liver, bladder, lungs, kidney, and prostate.

## FAMILIES, LARGE
When your kid asks for a baby sister, tell her she can't have one—for her own good. Children in large families have a heightened risk of developing Alzheimer's later in life.

## FAMILIES, SMALL
On the other hand, when she asks if you can send her baby brother back, don't go along with that either. Children in small families have a heightened risk of developing asthma and frequent wheezing later in childhood.

## FARMING (and see WORK)
Old MacDonald had a farm—and a lot of other things, too. Farming women who are exposed to pesticides may have an increased risk of breast cancer. Both men and women on farms

can suffer from pesticide-induced "mild cognitive dysfunctions" such as difficulties in speaking or problems in identifying words, colors, or numbers. Long-term use of organophosphates to treat sheep against parasites can damage the nervous system (which explains that glazed look sheep always have). Farmers also have unusually high rates of suicide and silicosis.

## FAT, BEING TOO (see also THIN, BEING TOO)

The "jolly fat person" is a myth; fat people have very little to laugh about. Obesity results in 300,000 deaths in the U.S. each year, and soon may overtake tobacco as the chief cause of preventable death in the United States. Being fat causes (or worsens) conditions like sleep apnea, osteoarthritis of the knee, shortness of breath, degenerative arthritis, cardiovascular disease, and gallstones, as well as a variety of cancers: one in ten fatal cancers affecting non-smokers is the result of obesity. The risk of diabetes increases by 4 percent for every pound of excess weight. Children who are overweight begin to feel a significant drop in self-esteem by the time they reach eighth grade, making them more likely to take up smoking and drinking; they also have a heightened risk of asthma and of artery damage that can lead to strokes and heart disease later in life. Overweight middle-aged men are more likely to have difficulty achieving erections, as well as to suffer from vascular dementia by the time they reach their late seventies. Seriously overweight women are 37 percent more likely than women of average weight to be clinically depressed during any given year—and this entry probably didn't help.

## FATHERS, OLD (see also MOTHERS, YOUNG)

The older a man is when he becomes a father, the more likely it is that his child will suffer from schizophrenia, cancer of the nervous system or prostate, dwarfism, malformation of the skull, hands, and feet, or Marfan syndrome, which involves defects of the eyes, bones, heart, and blood vessels. If you're ninety-five and your new baby is healthy and beautiful, congratulations— but maybe you need to have a little talk with your wife.

## FATIGUE (see also SHIFT WORK; SLEEP, TOO LITTLE)

Fatigue causes one in every ten car crashes ending in serious injury or death. And just to reassure you next time you're in the hospital: in one study, more than one-third of junior hospital doctors reported that their hours of duty were so long that their work was impaired.

## FEAR (see also MOODS)

If you're scared of surgery, skip this entry, because it's not going to help. People who are afraid of surgery tend to have excessive bleeding during their operations, as well as infections and complications afterwards.

## FEET, SMELLY (see also BODY)

If your feet smell, they'll probably end up itching too, since smelly feet attract *Anopheles gambiae* (a species of mosquito). And don't expect anyone to be around to sympathize, since smelly feet repel *Homo sapiens* (your girlfriend).

## FIBER, EATING (see also FOOD)

Dietary fiber, especially in the form of purified supplements, could increase your risk of developing colon cancer. They don't tell you that in the ads.

## FIBER, NOT EATING

On the other hand, not eating enough dietary fiber may increase your risk of cancer, heart disease, and obesity; and pregnant diabetics who consume too little fiber may need more insulin. Take your pick.

## FIREARMS (see GUNS; see also HUNTING)

## FIREWORKS (and see FOURTH OF JULY, HOLIDAYS)

Fireworks injure 8,500 people in the United States each year. Approximately 40 percent of these are children, which means at least 60 percent should have known better.

## FISH (see SEAFOOD; see also FOOD)

### FISHING

Women who eat sport fish from sources such as the Great Lakes, where there is contamination by polychlorinated biphenyls and persistent chlorinated pesticides, are less likely to be successful in becoming pregnant. If you like fish and don't like children, we guess this could be good news.

## FLOWER SHOPS (see also WORKPLACES)

Next time she complains that you don't bring her flowers anymore, tell her it's because it's just too much of a risk. Flower shops have high concentrations of molds, which can give you a stuffy nose, eye irritation, and wheezing. Prolonged exposure can lead to more severe reactions such as fever, shortness of breath, or mold infections in the lungs—so if you decide to buy her that bouquet after all, don't linger over your choice.

## FLOWERS (see also GRASS, TREES, WEEDS)

And giving someone flowers isn't necessarily a nice thing to do anyway, at least if they're in the hospital. Flowers in surgical wards increase the chances of patients being infected by a bacterium that develops in the water when the flowers rot in hot weather.

**FLU** (see INFLUENZA)

## FOLIC ACID, NOT TAKING

Women who don't take enough folic acid before and during pregnancy may be at greater risk of having children with childhood leukemia or spinal cord defects such as spina bifida. Considering what percentage of pregnancies are planned in advance, this information isn't quite as useful as it sounds, but we thought you'd like to know anyway.

## FOLIC ACID, TAKING

And here's the part they don't tell you on the vitamin bottle: folic acid can be double trouble. Women who take folic acid supplements during pregnancy double their chances of having twins, which are more likely to be premature, have low birthweights, and suffer from cerebral palsy.

## FOOD (see also ALFALFA SPROUTS, BREAD, CARROTS, CHEESES, CHINESE FOOD, CHOCOLATE, EATING, EGGS, ENERGY BARS, FIBER, FRUIT JUICE, LICORICE, MEALS, MEAT, MILK, NUTS, PEANUTS, PUMPKINS, RICE, SALT, SEAFOOD, SOYA BEANS, SWEETS, TUNA BURGERS, TURKEY, VEGETABLE OIL)

Contaminated food makes seventy-five million people sick and kills five thousand in the United States every year. You can avoid this by eating those unidentified vacuum-packed substances they give to astronauts, but most people who do this are scary individuals who live in bunkers and wait for the mother ship to come for them.

## FOOD, ETHNIC

Many popular ethnic foods, including all your favorites—sweet and sour pork with egg fried rice, crispy duck, lasagna, chicken tikka masala with pilaf rice, vegetable biryani, Tex-Mex food with sour cream and cheese, chicken enchiladas—contain unhealthy levels of fat. So stick with the traditional American health foods, like a Big Mac.

## FOOD, GENETICALLY MODIFIED (see BIOTECHNOLOGY)

## FOOD, IRRADIATED

There's a reason why nature doesn't normally irradiate things. Actually, there are a lot of reasons. According to Public Citizen, irradiation destroys vitamins, nutrients, and essential fatty acids; kills beneficial microorganisms; forms carcinogens in certain foods; creates free radicals that make the body more susceptible to cancer, diabetes, heart disease, liver damage, muscular breakdown, and other serious health problems; and (at least in laboratory animals) causes chromosomal damage, immune and reproductive problems, kidney damage, tumors, internal bleeding, low birthweight, and nutritional muscular dystrophy. Looks like you'd be better off going hungry.

## FOOD, NON-IRRADIATED

Non-irradiated foods are more likely to contain bacteria such as E. coli, campylobacter, and salmonella, and they spoil sooner. Given the alternative, though, salmonella is starting to look pretty tasty.

## FOOD, ORGANIC

Like so many things, it only tastes good if you don't think too hard about where it comes from. Organic farming relies on animal manure, which can contain deadly bacteria if it's not properly composted.

## FOOD, VEGETARIAN

If you're on a vegetarian diet when you get pregnant, you're less likely to give birth to a boy. (If you want a daughter, this is good news and belongs in a different book.) And if you do have a son, he's five times more likely to suffer from hypospadias, a condition in which the urethra opens below the tip of the penis. Vegetarians may suffer loss of sexual function, while vegan diets deficient in minerals and vitamins can lead to blindness.

## FOOD AID (and see BIOTECHNOLOGY)

Genetically modified corn distributed as food aid to poor Mexican peasants may have contaminated local species, threatening the invaluable genetic diversity of native strains. The World Food Program plans to solve the problem by giving the Mexicans genetically modified wheat.

## FOOD COLORING

Artificial food colorings may be linked to attention-deficit hyperactivity disorder, whose symptoms include reduced attentiveness and concentration, excessive levels of activity, distractibility, and impulsiveness. Any parent who's ever let the kids eat candy too close to bedtime could have told you this without a lot of expensive research.

## FOOTBALL (see also SPORTS)

Football

Football players are prone to acne mechanica and to injury of the medial and lateral collateral ligaments. Also—this may or may not come as a surprise—20 percent of high school players and 10 percent of college players suffer brain injuries each year. More than half of all professional football players suffer concussions during their careers; this can lead to later problems with memory and concentration, confusion, speech or hearing difficulties, numbness or tingling in extremities, and headaches.

## FORMULA FEEDING (see BOTTLE-FEEDING)

## FOURTH OF JULY (see FIREWORKS and HOLIDAYS)

### FRIENDS (see also ISOLATION)

When your best friend says, "I'll be there for you," think twice before taking her up on it. A study found that women giving a difficult speech suffered more stress when a friend was present.

### FRUIT JUICE (see also DRINKS)

Unpasteurized fruit juices can be contaminated by E. coli (which can lead to hemolytic uremic syndrome, a severe blood and kidney disorder), listeria monocytogenes (a pathogen that can harm pregnant women), and salmonella. On the other hand, consider the alternatives: COFFEE, MILK, SOFT DRINKS, TEA, WATER...

### FURNITURE WORKER, BEING A (and see WORK)

Save the children: buy a brand-new chair. Workers stripping old paint from furniture can carry enough dust home on their clothing to give their children lead poisoning.

### GAMBLING

If you're a so-called "pathological gambler," you're raising your risk of becoming dependent on cocaine and/or tobacco, showing signs of antisocial personality disorder, being unemployed, participating in illegal activities, and being incarcerated. But you're probably willing to take the gamble.

### GARBAGE BAGS

Garbage bags attract rats, which easily chew through the plastic. Some cities, including New York, are thinking of requiring that all garbage be enclosed in heavy cans for collection. (In New York, the rats would probably just make off with the garbage cans.)

## GARBAGE COLLECTOR, BEING A (and see WORK)

Garbage collectors have an unusually high risk of dying from pulmonary tuberculosis. Also, nobody will sit next to them on the bus.

## GARDENING (see also POTTING SOIL)

You think you've got a green thumb, but do too much gardening and you might not be so sure. Gardeners exposed to pesticides are five times more likely than the general population to suffer from so-called "mild cognitive dysfunctions" such as difficulties in speaking or problems in identifying words, numbers, or colors. So was that thumb green, or purple, or...

## GARDENING, TV PROGRAMS ON (see also DO IT YOURSELF, TV PROGRAMS ON)

Green thumbs can also turn into sore thumbs. People get inspired by TV programs on gardening and overextend themselves in their own gardens, risking damage to their backs, shoulders, and hands.

## GARLIC, NOT TAKING

People who take don't take garlic supplements are at higher risk of malaria and cancer, and are much more likely to come down with colds. They're also more likely to be bitten by vampires.

## GARLIC, TAKING

Garlic supplements sharply reduce the effectiveness of at least one anti-HIV drug. On the other hand, they make you less likely to get HIV in the first place: nobody's going to get that close to you if you've been eating garlic.

## GAS, COOKING WITH

Fumes given off by gas cooking may result in or aggravate respiratory problems. Finally, a good use for that gas mask you bought in September 2001.

### GAS STATIONS (see also WORKPLACES)

Believe it or not, being a gas station attendant isn't as much fun as it looks. People working in gas stations are subject to an unusually high rate of homicides.

### GENETICALLY MODIFIED FOOD (see BIOTECHNOLOGY)

### GINKGO BILOBA (see also CHINESE MEDICINES, HERBAL REMEDIES)

Ginkgo biloba acts as a blood thinner and may increase the risk of excessive bleeding or stroke if taken with anticoagulant drugs. (This is the pharmaceutical industry's version; the Chinese healer's version is that anticoagulant drugs are bad for you.)

## GLOBAL WARMING

According to some politicians, global warming is a myth. Just the same, that myth is going to increase disease and death all over the world as a result of heat waves, respiratory problems, drowning, hurricanes, starvation, and the spread of infectious diseases ranging from malaria to dengue fever—but keep telling yourself it's not really happening. Agriculture will become impossible in some areas, and many of the world's forests will die—but don't worry, that'll just be your imagination. More than half of the terrestrial habitat may be lost in some areas, and up to 20 percent of local species of plants and animals may be forced into extinction—but we won't miss them, right? Allergies may increase, because there will be more ragweed pollen in the air—but remind yourself it's only a myth that you're sneezing. Some parts of the world are likely to become uninsurable—but hey, anyone rich enough to matter has plenty of property in the other parts. It's already starting: polar bears are in trouble because the sea ice on which they hunt for food is disappearing; the Antarctic's emperor penguin population has fallen by half; Australia's Great Barrier Reef is experiencing "bleaching" that hints at its eventual destruction; and global warming has been blamed for a sharp worldwide decline in the numbers of frogs, toads, and salamanders—but who needs them anyway?

## GO-CARTS

An average of 10,500 people, mostly children, are treated in U.S. emergency rooms each year, and at least twenty die, as a result of go-cart injuries. Stop cart.

### GOLF (see also SPORTS, TIGER WOODS)

Forget about closing that nice little deal over the eighth hole. One-fourth to one-third of golfers have been injured playing the game. Common problems include lower back injuries, pinched nerves, tears of the rotator cuff, medial epicondylitis, carpal tunnel syndrome, and spinal damage. Golfers are also susceptible to skin cancers because of exposure to the sun.

### GRASS (see also FLOWERS, TREES, WEEDS)

Allergic reactions can be caused by various grasses including timothy, Bermuda, orchard, red top, and sweet vernal. Enjoy your picnic.

### GUM DISEASE (see also DISEASES)

Keep flossing. People with gum disease may have a heightened risk of chronic obstructive pulmonary disease and diabetes.

### GUNS (see also HUNTING)

In 1997 alone, there were 32,436 firearm-related deaths in the U.S. (which is, of course, a small price to pay for the right to shoot possums in your backyard), with 4,223 of the victims being younger than twenty years of age. In the U.S., the rate of firearm-related deaths for children under fifteen is twelve times higher than in other industrialized countries, and the overall rate of firearm-related homicide is nearly sixteen times higher. Tonight on *The X-Files*, Scully investigates: as we all know that guns don't kill people, *what killed these people*? Could it be aliens? The CIA? A rare virus? The truth is out there...

### GYMNASTICS (see also SPORTS)

Among sports played by physical education students, gymnastics has the highest rate of injuries. And when you wince watching male gymnasts doing the splits, you're right: pelvic injuries suffered during gymnastics can lead to impotence in men.

### HAIR DYES

Stick with your distinguished gray. Use of permanent hair dyes may cause bladder cancer.

### HAIRDRESSER, BEING A (and see WORK)

When your six-year-old offers to cut your hair like she cut her Barbie's, let her—for your hairdresser's sake. Hairdressers are at unusually high risk of contracting bladder cancer, and may develop allergic contact dermatitis from the chemicals with which they work.

### HALLOWEEN (and see HOLIDAYS)

Four times as many children aged five to fourteen are killed while walking on Halloween evening compared with other evenings, and many are injured in falls. The latex in Halloween masks can give some children rashes, asthma attacks, or other allergic reactions. Trick or treat!

## HANGOVERS (see also DRINKING)

Hangovers may increase the risk of cardiac death (which, if your hangover is bad enough, may not seem like such a terrible idea) and can produce cognitive and visual-spatial impairments that are hazardous in some kinds of work.

## HEADACHES

Children who have frequent headaches are more likely to have physical and mental health problems when they grow up. Of course, this could have something to do with what's giving them the headaches.

## HEADS, BALD (see also BODY)

Bald men are more likely to develop heart disease than men with hair. And no, hair plugs will not help, but nice try.

## HEADS, ROUND

People with round heads are more likely to have serious snoring problems. That's why, when the little red-haired girl moved in with Charlie Brown, she moved right back out again....

## HEADS, SMALL

If you carry the APOE e4 gene, which puts you at risk for Alzheimer's, having a small head makes it three times more likely that you will actually get the disease. Take that bicycle pump out of your ear.

## HEALTH

For the good of your health, get sick. If you're healthy, your immune system is underused, so it may overreact to minor threats, producing antibody molecules that release inflammatory substances in your lungs and cause asthma.

## HEART ATTACKS

From our Adding-Insult-to-Injury Department: after a heart attack, many survivors then suffer from post-traumatic stress disorder as a result of the attack.

## HEART BYPASS SURGERY (see BYPASS SURGERY)

## HEELS, HIGH

Women who wear stilettos or (even worse) broad high heels such as court shoes risk developing crippling osteoarthritis in the knee. Then again, short women can only see the top half of concerts, and they never get served in crowded bars. Your call.

## HERBAL REMEDIES (see also CHINESE MEDICINES, ECHINACEA, ENERGY BARS, GINKGO BILOBA, EPHEDRA, ST. JOHN'S WORT, WEIGHT-LOSS PRODUCTS)

Sure, they're natural, but Mother Nature is not a nice lady. If taken before surgery, St. John's wort and kava-kava could prolong the sedative effect of anesthesia; ginkgo biloba, garlic, ginger, and ginseng may prevent blood clots from forming and therefore lead to excess bleeding; ephedra can result in cardiovascular instability; ginseng can result in hypoglycemia; and you can injure your liver through high doses of germander, chaparral leaf, comfrey, jin bu huan, ma huang, valerian, mistletoe, or pennyroyal, as well as kava-kava, which has been linked with cases of liver failure in Europe.

## HERPES (and see SEX)

Children of mothers with genital herpes may be at greater risk of schizophrenia and other psychotic illnesses when they grow up.

That could be due to the lingering presence of the guy who gave her herpes in the first place.

## HIGH CHAIRS (see also BABY CARE)

During 1999, 6,600 children under the age of five were injured in the U.S. when they fell out of high chairs. You can try supergluing the kid to the seat, but this often leads to technical difficulties in changing diapers.

## HIGH SCHOOL (see also SCHOOLS)

This won't come as news to anyone over fourteen: high school sucks. In a recent study, half of high school students who belonged to organized groups said they'd been subjected to hazing, including being yelled or cursed at, told to miss school, forced to drink alcohol or use illegal drugs, or made to vandalize property, cheat, or engage in sexual acts. (Back when we were in high school, we didn't need to be forced to drink alcohol, engage in sexual acts, and the rest of it, but maybe times have changed.)

## HOCKEY (see also SPORTS)

Playing ice hockey can lead to fracture or dislocation of the spine, head injuries resulting in neurological deficit (particularly among sixteen- to twenty-year-old players), and injuries to the medial and lateral collateral ligaments. You also aren't likely to be left with any TEETH (which actually could be a good thing—keep reading).

## HOLIDAYS (see also CHRISTMAS, FOURTH OF JULY, HALLOWEEN, NEW YEAR, THANKSGIVING, VALENTINE'S DAY; and see CAMPING, BEACH ITEMS, BEACHES, FIREWORKS, MOUNTAINS, PACKAGE HOLIDAYS)

Never mind "'tis the season to be jolly": holidays can actually depress you. Unrealistic expectations, too much commercialization, stress, and fatigue from shopping, parties, family reunions, or houseguests—all these can trigger sadness and depression. If you've lost a loved one, holidays can make you feel even worse. To add injury to insult, summer holiday cottages have high concentrations of molds, which can cause nasal stuffiness, eye irritation, wheezing, or (through prolonged exposure) more severe reactions such as fever, shortness of breath, or mold infections in the lungs.

## HOLY WATER
And now, today's test of faith: students who analyzed holy water in church fonts for a Young Scientist contest in Ireland found dirt, coliforms, staphylococcus, yeasts, molds, and tiny green worms. So, does the holiness neutralize the nasty things, or not?

### HOMELESSNESS (see also HOMES)
Suicide rates are unusually high among the homeless. The scientific term for this kind of observation is 'duh.'

### HOMES (see also HOMELESSNESS; and see BEDDING, CARPETS, DUST)
If you're reading this at home, maybe you should take a deep breath—or not. The air in homes may be polluted by gas, tobacco smoke, carbon monoxide, asbestos, cleaning materials, radon, pesticides, and substances from damp carpets or pressed wood products, leading to a wide range of health problems. Exposure to carcinogens is likely to be much greater

Home

than outside the home: for example, average levels of exposure to benzene, a known carcinogen, are three times as high indoors as outdoors. Home sweet home.

## HOMES, COLD AND DAMP

Living in a cold, damp house can lead to premature death, physical and mental illness, and impaired quality of life. No, this does not mean that GLOBAL WARMING is your friend.

## HOMES, NEW

Studies in the U.K. and Australia found that people in new homes were exposed to very high levels of carcinogenic chemicals such as formaldehyde and styrene leaking into the air out of carpets, floors, and paints. Real estate agents being what they are, they probably charged you extra for that new-house smell.

## HOMES, OLD

And guess what? That doesn't mean it's good news if you're too broke to buy a new house. Houses built before 1950 are likely to have lead-based paints that can give children lead poisoning. In America, 4.4 percent of children have dangerous levels of lead in their blood, often resulting in damage to the central nervous system, a decrease in IQ, attention deficit disorder, behavioral disturbances, and other problems.

## HOMES IN THE WOODS

People who built houses with large yards in wooded areas accounted for a sharp increase in cases of Lyme disease in the late 1990s. This probably wasn't included in your vision of your romantic woodland getaway.

## HOMOSEXUALITY

Even if you don't believe what the televangelists say (and you shouldn't), homosexuality is bad for you. Suicide rates for young lesbians and gay men are considerably higher than the rates for heterosexuals. On the other hand, SEX of any kind is bad for you, anyway.

## HORMONE REPLACEMENT THERAPY (see also
### ESTROGEN, PRESCRIPTION DRUGS)

Hormone replacement therapy is associated with an increased risk of asthma and recurrent major coronary events. Anyway, think about it: this is the hormone that once made you kiss a Donny Osmond poster good night. Why would you want it back?

## HORSEBACK RIDING (see also SPORTS)

Mamas, don't let your babies grow up to be cowboys: men can become impotent from riding horses. Like the song says, "they're always alone, even with someone they love." (So why were the women the ones who rode sidesaddle?)

## HOSPITALS (see also EMERGENCY ROOMS, INTENSIVE
### CARE, MEDICAL PROCEDURES)

Now here's one you didn't expect: hospitals are bad for you. Medical errors in hospitals kill between forty-eight thousand and ninety-eight thousand people and injure a million more each year in the U.S. Errors in medications alone affect one patient in twenty. In addition, infections acquired in hospitals affect approximately two million people annually (a rate of infection up 36 percent in the past twenty years), and are among the leading causes of death in the United States. In the U.K., a study found that more than one patient in every ten admitted to a hospital suffered some sort of harm while there, from minor infections to death, as a result of drugs being injected in the wrong part of the body. And (figure this one out) patients who have a stroke while in a hospital are more likely to die than patients who are admitted following a stroke.

## HOSTILITY (see also ANGER)

Young adults who score high on measures of hostility are 2.5 times more likely than less hostile people to have heart disease ten years later. This is known as "karma."

## HOTEL CLERK, BEING A (and see WORK)

Hotel clerks have unusually high rates of death from homicide and asthma. On convention days, these could feel like blessings.

## HOUSEBOATS

Seventy-four people suffered carbon monoxide poisoning, and seven of these died, while standing or swimming near houseboat swim platforms during the 1990s at Lake Powell, on the Arizona-Utah border. You'd think that after the first twenty or thirty collapsed, the others would have found somewhere else to swim.

## HOUSING, PUBLIC

People who live in public housing have more than double the normal risk of being victims of handgun violence. If you've ever seen the luxuries of public housing, you'll understand: you'd feel like shooting someone, too.

## HOUSING, STUDENT

Student housing, which tends to be cheap and is therefore often dank and moldy, can significantly increase an undergraduate's risk of asthma, pneumonia, and bronchitis. If you're living a typical undergraduate life, though, this won't affect you much, because you'll only see your place every few weeks.

### HOUSTON (and see CITIES)

Houston, you have a problem. Houston is the fattest city in America.

### HUNTING (see also GUNS)

The risk of having marked hearing loss increases 7 percent for every five years a person has hunted. But remember, guns don't cause deafness; people cause deafness.

## HUTTERITE, BEING A

Hutterites in Canada were found to have more neurotic disorders than the general population. (Warning to both Canadian Hutterites reading this book: seek help.)

## INCENSE

Does incense help you meditate? Not any more, it won't. Incense fumes contain chemicals that are associated with lung, bladder, skin, and scrotal cancers, thus doing bad things to several of your chakras. Ommmmm.

### INCINERATORS (see also DIOXINS)

Incinerators used to dispose of municipal wastes produce large amounts of toxic ash and release heavy metals (such as lead, cadmium, arsenic, mercury, and chromium) as well as chemicals such as dioxins into the environment. If you live near an incinerator, or even if you just eat food crops that have been grown too near an incinerator, you can end up with increased cancer rates, respiratory ailments, reproductive abnormalities, and plenty of other health effects. Better use a LANDFILL instead.

### INDIA (see also AMERICA, CHINA, DOMINICAN REPUBLIC, EGYPT, KENYA, MEXICO, PERU, TUNISIA)

Next stop on our wonderful world tour: the ashrams, the Taj Mahal, the Ganges, the bacteria…In that study, 41 percent of the tourists who traveled to India got sick.

### INFANT CARRIERS (see also BABY CARE)

Get a babysitter and leave the kid at home. During 1999, 12,820 children under the age of five were injured in falls from infant carriers and car seats.

## INFLUENZA (see also DISEASES)

More scary information you can't do anything with: if you have the flu during the second trimester of pregnancy, there's an increased risk that your child will someday suffer from schizophrenia.

## INFORMATION TECHNOLOGY (see also COMPUTERS, INTERNET)

In the U.S., the pressure of mastering the information technology revolution is one of the main causes of the high rates of depression, stress, and burnout in the workplace. This is known as "progress."

## INSECTICIDES (see also PESTICIDES)

Maybe you should start learning to love your mosquito bites. Using insecticides in the home may double your risk of developing Parkinson's disease. Automatic insecticide dispensers used in restaurants and other businesses have been linked to illnesses such as sore throats, headaches, dizziness, irritation of the eyes and lungs, nausea, and diarrhea.

## INTELLIGENCE, HIGH

Don't be too pleased if you find out your kid's a genius. Children with high intelligence may become bored, tune out, underachieve, become depressed, feel alienated from their classmates, be targeted for teasing, or be incorrectly diagnosed as hyperactive.

## INTELLIGENCE, LOW

On the other hand, don't celebrate if your kid's not the brightest pixie in the forest, either. Children with low IQs are more likely to be delinquent teens and criminal adults, and they die sooner. People with lower intelligence are more likely to get Alzheimer's and to suffer from post-traumatic stress disorder if they have a traumatic experience.

## INTENSIVE CARE (see also EMERGENCY ROOMS, HOSPITALS, MEDICAL DIAGNOSES)

A study has found that one-fifth of people who died in an intensive care unit had been misdiagnosed, and that in 44 percent of these cases, a correct diagnosis would have resulted in different treatment. (The medical term for this is "D'oh!") If they put you on a mechanical ventilator in the ICU, you have one chance in ten of developing ventilator-associated pneumonia.

## INTERNET (see also COMPUTERS, INFORMATION TECHNOLOGY)

Doctors face an epidemic of "cyberchondria," in which patients look up their symptoms on the Internet and misdiagnose themselves. Much of the health information on the Internet is hard to find, hard to read, and often incorrect or incomplete with respect to a wide range of conditions, including skin and breast cancer, childhood asthma, depression, obesity, and carpal tunnel syndrome. Plus, according to one expert, surfing through the Net looking for stuff like this can leave you with an attention span of nine seconds, the same as a goldfish's. One final note: that hot twenty-year-old lap-dancer in the chat room is actually a weird fortysomething guy who hasn't left his room since 1994.

## INTERNET FILTERING SOFTWARE

Bet you hadn't guessed what the *real* new threat to your freedom is. Software that lets you filter the news you receive on the Internet according to your personal interests may narrow your mind, make your views more extreme, and undercut democracy.

Look out for *Rambo 12: Shattered Software*, coming soon to a cinema near you.

## ISOLATION (see also FRIENDS)
Your chances of sickness and death are doubled if you feel socially isolated, making isolation a risk factor greater than cigarette smoking. (Since smokers are socially isolated anyway these days, they're in real trouble.) Isolation also increases the risk of dementia.

## JANITOR, BEING A (and see WORK)
Janitors have an unusually high risk of dying of silicosis. We have no idea why.

## JOGGING (see also SPORTS)
The more you jog, the more likely you are to suffer knee pain from conditions such as tendon injuries or chondromalacia. That sound you hear is millions of non-joggers snickering.

## KENYA (see also AMERICA, CHINA, DOMINICAN REPUBLIC, EGYPT, INDIA, MEXICO, PERU, TUNISIA)
Time for our Safari Special! Got your camera, your Swahili phrasebook, and your medical insurance? In our favorite study of tourists, nearly half of those who traveled to Kenya got sick.

## LABELING, FOOD PACKAGE
Don't believe everything you read. In describing the ingredients in food on package labels, one manufacturer in four fails to mention items that can cause potentially fatal allergic reactions.

## LANDFILLS
Because of all the bad things INCINERATORS do, we suggested landfills instead, right? We've changed our minds. A study in the

U.K. found that women who live within a mile of a landfill have an increased risk of giving birth to babies with problems such as spina bifida, holes in the heart, or (in the case of boys) genital defects.

## LATE NIGHTS (see SHIFT WORK)

## LAUGHING
Muscles weaken when people laugh, possibly leading in extreme cases to a form of narcolepsy. We hope you don't find this funny.

## LAUGHING, NOT
If you don't laugh enough, you're more likely to have heart disease. Unfortunately, this isn't funny either.

## LEFT-HANDED, BEING
Postmenopausal women who are left-handed are more likely to get breast cancer. Left-handers are particularly subject to repetitive strain injury, since equipment tends to be designed by right-handed designers for right-handed users—everything from scissors to those annoying one-piece desks is always made for righties. Left-handers are also more likely to get inflammatory bowel disease and to have birth or pregnancy complications; they're more susceptible to conditions such as diabetes and epilepsy; and they're more likely to be alcoholics (which is odd, since corkscrews are always right-handed) and criminals. As a result, left-handers live for nine years less than right-handers.

## LEGS, RESTLESS (see also BODY)
Restless Leg Syndrome, which occurs in 6 percent of the adult population (no, we are not making this up), is strongly correlated with poor physical and mental health, in part because symptoms may keep the sufferer awake.

## LEGS, SHORT (see also BODY; SHORT, BEING)

Men with short legs are more likely to get heart disease and diabetes. They also have trouble finding pants that fit.

## LIBRARIAN, BEING A (and see WORK)

Librarians have an unusually high risk of dying from asthma. This actually sounds fairly appealing, compared with a lifetime of supervising teenaged boys as they surf the Web for Britney in a bikini.

## LICORICE

Licorice can raise your blood pressure and may decrease testosterone levels and libido. At last, a contraceptive nobody's embarrassed to be seen buying!

## LIGHT, ELECTRIC

Electric Light

Using electric lights at night could suppress your body's production of melatonin and increase your risk of breast cancer. Care to live by candlelight instead? Yeah, right: see CANDLES.

## LIPOSUCTION (see also MEDICAL PROCEDURES)

And the front-runner for the Elvis Award for the Least Dignified Way to Die: liposuction (the way Elvis himself might have died if he'd lived long enough to try it). According to one survey of plastic surgeons, the death rate for liposuction is twenty to sixty times higher than the death rate for all operations performed in hospitals.

## LIQUOR STORES (see also WORKPLACES)

People working in liquor stores suffer the second-highest rate of occupational homicides. And it's not even worth it—they almost never get employee discounts.

## LOS ANGELES (and see CITIES, TRAFFIC)

In a survey of sixty-eight cities, Los Angeles had the worst traffic, with half of daily travel taking place in congested conditions. At least when the Big One comes, you'll already be in your car.

## LOUISIANA (see also NEW ORLEANS, STATES)

Louisiana is the second most unhealthy state in the U.S. It would probably be around number five if it weren't for the Mardi Gras festival.

## LYING

When you tell a lie, more blood is pumped into your nasal tissues—so your nose gets longer. This condition is technically known as acute pinocchiosis.

## MAN, BEING A (see also WOMAN)

At any age, men are more likely to die than women. (It's possible that women actually live forever, but we won't be around to find out.) Boys are up to ten times as likely as girls to have Asperger's Syndrome, baby boys are more susceptible to childhood illness, young men die more frequently than women in road and other accidents, and older men die more often from industrial injuries and cardiovascular disease. Men are four times as likely as women to kill themselves, and twice as likely to get Parkinson's disease. Men get oral and bladder cancer two to three times as often as women do and are more likely to be late in seeking treatment for melanomas, making prospects for successful treatment less favorable. Men are slower than women to recover from coronary artery disease and are more likely to sicken or die from the effects of social isolation. Ladies, are you feeling sorry for these poor creatures by now? We didn't think so.

## MARATHONS (see RUNNING)

## MARIJUANA (see also COCAINE, DRINKING, ECSTASY)

If you smoke marijuana, your risk of a heart attack quintuples for an hour after you light up; for the period after that, it stays at twice the normal risk. This may or may not be because you ate two double-cheese pizzas and that weird stuff from the back of the fridge.

## MARIJUANA USERS

Young men who smoke marijuana are five times as likely to be violent as those who don't. (We find this pretty odd, considering that when we're stoned we can't even get irritated, never mind get up; but we suppose you could stretch far enough to hit someone with the pizza box if he was really messing with your head.) We're currently planning a small-scale study to test these findings; we'll let you know how it turns out, if we remember.

## MARRIAGE (see also UNMARRIED, BEING)

Quarreling with your spouse can have a bad effect on your immune system, causing colds and upper respiratory infections. (This gives you another thing to fight about: whose fault is your head cold?) Unhappily married women also have a high risk of dying from cardiovascular disease, giving new meaning to the term "heartbreak."

## MARRIAGE: IN THE ELDERLY

And they lived happily ever after…for a while. Among the elderly, there are special risks in marriage, since an intimate relationship can be particularly harmful when it goes wrong. Older women who argue with their husbands can experience hormonal changes, and the immune systems of both husband and wife can suffer, leaving them more prone to infections and slower to heal. You're better off just having close friends.

## MEALS, LARGE
### (see also FOOD)
Remember this one as you're enjoying your delicious Thanksgiving dinner: having an unusually large meal increases your risk of a heart attack tenfold in the hour after eating. Mmm…large.

## MEAT, PRODUCING
The world's meat production is expected to go up by 50 percent over the next twenty years. This will force animal and human populations closer together, especially in the developing world, thus aiding the spread of disease as bacteria and viruses are passed back and forth. Got your foot-and-mouth vaccination yet?

## MEAT, EATING (see also FOOD)
Polishing off that giant steak down at Cowboy Joe's may feel like a macho thing to do, but not for long. Eating red meat can give you cancer of the prostate, colon, and rectum. Diets rich in animal fat may also increase your risk of esophageal and stomach cancers.

## MEAT, EATING WELL-COOKED (see also FOOD)
Women who regularly eat well-done hamburger, steak, and bacon have a risk of breast cancer 4.6 times higher than women who eat those meats cooked rare or medium. And you thought it all went straight to your thighs.

## MECHANIC, BEING A (and see WORK)
Mechanics who work with hydrocarbon solvents such as petrol or rubber are at risk of developing Parkinson's disease and may

suffer from allergic contact dermatitis. On the other hand, you get more opportunities to mess with people's minds ("Well, it's either your spark plugs or your fan belt or maybe something else; come back in six weeks") than anyone except doctors and maybe construction workers.

## MEDIA, THE (see also MEDICAL JOURNALS, PRESCRIPTION DRUGS)

A study of media coverage of new drugs found that 53 percent of news reports failed to disclose drug risks; 40 percent described benefits without any statistical context, such as a person's actual risk of getting a particular disease; 70 percent failed to mention the drug's cost-effectiveness; and 61 percent failed to reveal when the experts being quoted had financial ties to drug makers. You have to wonder what else they're leaving out. (Rumor has it that life on Mars was discovered in 1984, but it happened the same week as Michael Jackson's head transplant, so the media missed it.)

## MEDICAL DIAGNOSES (see also DOCTORS, INTENSIVE CARE, PRESCRIPTION DRUGS)

In 40 percent of cases, autopsies reveal a major misdiagnosis by doctors of the patient's condition; in about one-third of these cases, the patients would have lived if proper treatment had been given. Comfortingly, though, the other two-thirds didn't have a chance anyway.

## MEDICAL JOURNALS (see also MEDIA)

Fewer than 40 percent of reports on drug trials in medical journals adequately explain the severity of side effects, and fewer than 30 percent adequately explain drug toxicity. This means your doctor knows as little as you do about the medicines he's prescribing. But look on the bright side; at least you won't be surprised when you read what happens when you take PRE-SCRIPTION DRUGS.

## MEDICAL PROCEDURES (see BYPASS SURGERY; CHEMOTHERAPY; CIRCUMCISED, BEING; LIPOSUCTION; ORGAN TRANSPLANTS)

## MEDICINE (see OVER-THE-COUNTER DRUGS, PRESCRIPTION DRUGS)

## MEN
One-and-a-half million reasons to become a nun: more than 1.5 million women each year in the U.S. are subjected to physical or sexual violence by a boyfriend, husband, or date.

## MENSTRUAL CYCLE
Female athletes are more likely to suffer an anterior cruciate ligament injury during the ovulatory phase of their menstrual cycle, and women who suffer from migraines are twice as likely to have one during the first two days of their period than during the rest of the month. The only advantage anyone has come up with is that you get to skip gym class every month.

## MEXICO (see also AMERICA, CHINA, DOMINICAN REPUBLIC, EGYPT, INDIA, KENYA, PERU, TUNISIA)
Next on our world tour (for those of you who are still standing): the Halls of Montezuma—or, for many of you, the Stalls of Montezuma. More than three in ten of those tourists who traveled to Mexico got sick.

## MIAMI (and see CITIES, TRAFFIC)
In a study of sixty-eight American cities, Miami was eleventh worst in terms of road traffic, with 47 percent of daily travel

taking place in congested conditions. Not only that, you need a phrasebook of Spanish slang just to figure out what the other drivers are yelling at you (rule of thumb: anything containing the words "tu madre" is not good).

## MICE (and see ANIMALS)

Mouse

In inner cities of the U.S., 95 percent of homes were found to have at least one room containing mouse allergen, which can cause severe asthma in one child in five. The traditional solution is to get a cat, but you should probably see CATS first.

## MIDDLE CLASS, BEING

The Americans most susceptible to post-traumatic stress disorder after the attacks in New York and Washington in September 2001 were members of the middle class. The poor were less stunned by the discovery that the world is not a safe place.

## MIDWEST, THE (see also EAST, SOUTH, WEST)

The Midwest is second only to the West as the region of the U.S. with the highest rate of crimes against person and property. It's second only to the South as the region with the highest rate of stroke deaths after hospital release. Not only that, global warming is going to lower water levels in the Great Lakes, leading to reduced water supplies and more costly transportation—but hey, don't worry about it: WATER and TRAVEL are both bad for you anyway, and GLOBAL WARMING doesn't really exist.

## MILK, DRINKING (see also CALCIUM, TAKING; DRINKS)

And now, the part they didn't tell you in those cute little milk-moustache ads. You know about lactose intolerance, but did you know that consuming lots of dairy products can increase your risk of prostate cancer? Also, very young children with a diabetic parent may develop antibodies to insulin if they're fed cow's milk, increasing the chance that they'll become diabetic themselves.

## MILK, NOT DRINKING (see also CALCIUM, NOT TAKING; DRINKS)
Not drinking milk deprives children of vitamins A, B, C, and D, calcium, magnesium, and phosphorus, all of which are necessary for growth and development. Put that milk moustache back on.

## MINER, BEING A (and see WORK)
Miners suffer from an unusually high incidence of asbestosis, coal workers' pneumoconiosis, malignant neoplasm of the pleura, and chronic obstructive pulmonary disease. They also run up huge bills at the laundromat and the canary store.

## MINING
Toxic cadmium from abandoned mines in Colorado is destroying the bones of the white-tailed ptarmigan and may also affect other birds, deer, elk, moose, rabbits, beaver, and possibly people. Environmental protection agencies are looking into this and will have a full report sometime between February and 2058.

## MISSISSIPPI (and see STATES)
Mississippi is the most unhealthy state in the U.S. This is why everyone who's left is singing the blues.

## MOBILE PHONES (see CELL PHONES)

## MOLD
Toxic molds from water damage in homes and offices can give off substances such as mycotoxins that lead to respiratory, skin,

and cognitive problems. And molds are second only to pollens as a cause of airborne allergies. They make great biology projects for your little brother, though.

## MONEY (see COINS, DOLLAR BILLS)

## MOODS (see ANGER, ANXIETY, EMOTIONAL RESTRAINT, FEAR, HOSTILITY, OPENNESS, OPTIMISM, PESSIMISM, SELF-ESTEEM, SHYNESS)

## MOON, THE
At the new moon, people are more likely to commit suicide. At the full moon, you're more likely to be bitten by animals, especially werewolves.

## MOTHBALLS
Many mothballs contain the chemical compound 1,4-dichlorobenzene, which is a suspected carcinogen. Well, most of us had already figured they couldn't be good for you, or how would they get rid of moths?

## MOTHERS, OLD (see also MOTHERS, YOUNG)
Don't wait too long to start that family: if they're born to older mothers, first children are more likely to develop diabetes before the age of fifteen.

## MOTHERS, TALL
Researchers have found that children of mothers taller than 5' 4" are twice as likely as children of mothers shorter than 4' 11" to fracture their hips when they grow up. Since tall mothers have tall daughters, who grow up to be tall women, who we already knew (see TALL, BEING) get more hip fractures, it seems probable that these researchers spent most of their grant money on

beer and pizza. We are currently applying for government funding to research this hypothesis.

## MOTHERS, YOUNG (see also MOTHERS, OLD; FATHERS, OLD)

Don't start that family too early, either: children of teenaged mothers are twice as likely to commit crimes. (Given what the children of older fathers are like, the perfect child—except for its diabetes—would have to have an old mother and a young father; so why do movies always show old men getting together with twenty-year-old girls?)

## MOUNTAINS (and see HOLIDAYS)

A study of people vacationing in the Colorado mountains found that 15 to 40 percent fall victim to mountain sickness, including major conditions such as high-altitude cerebral edema or pulmonary edema. Is "because it's there" *really* a good enough reason?

## MOVIES (see also COMPUTER GAMES, TELEVISION, VIDEO GAMES)

More than one thousand studies show a causal relationship between violence in the media (including movies) and aggressive behavior in children, with measurable and long-lasting effects including emotional desensitization toward real-life violence. No, this does not mean you can sue Steven Spielberg because your daughter has been biting her little brother ever since she saw *Jurassic Park IV*.

## MOVIE STARS

Teenagers are more likely to smoke if movie stars they admire smoke on screen. Ban *Casablanca* and keep them on a diet of *Forrest Gump* and *Rambo*: they may end up stupid and homicidal, but at least they won't smoke.

## MOVING AROUND

The shorter the time you've lived in your current residence, the more likely you are to be a victim of violent crime. Play the odds: stay inside and don't unlock your door for the first year or two.

## MULTITASKING

Multitasking may mean that none of the multi tasks get done properly. It may also erode your ability to focus, persevere, and be patient, reflective, or tranquil.

## MUNITIONS PLANTS, WORKING AT

Workers exposed to toxic chemicals at a munitions plant were found to have reduced psychomotor speed, diminished manual dexterity and auditory verbal recall, and disturbance of emotional and visual function. People exposed to the munitions were even worse off.

### MUSICIAN, BEING A

**(and see WORK)**

Musicians are at risk for repetitive motion conditions including carpal tunnel syndrome and tendonitis, hearing loss, upper extremity musculoskeletal problems, dermatitis and other skin conditions resulting from holding instruments, and second-hand smoke exposure, as well as performance anxiety and sleep disturbances. It has not yet been proven that any or all of these conditions have anything to do with groupies, but dedicated researchers are working hard to find out.

## NEVADA (and see STATES)
Nevada is the sixth most unhealthy state in the U.S. (and it's not just because of FALLON). But most of the residents seem to be willing to take their chances.

## NEW ORLEANS (and see CITIES, LOUISIANA)
Over a ten-year period, New Orleans had the third highest murder rate among large American cities. It's also the fourth fattest city in America. Every now and then, someone yells, "Yo, big mama!" once too often...

## NEW YEAR (see also HOLIDAYS)
A study in Australia found that the highest incidence of dog bites requiring hospital admission was on New Year's Day. It didn't say whether this was linked to the way Australians sound singing "Auld Lang Syne" after eight or nine pints.

## NEW YORK (and see CITIES)
If this was ever funny, it isn't any more: New York attracts crazies the way a flower attracts bees. It has also been called the nation's asthma capital (among other, less flattering things) and has the highest number of deaths of any city as a result of pollution from power plants. New Yorkers were the first in the U.S. to contract West Nile viral encephalitis. Plus, there's no place to park your car. Now that the Internet lets you work from anyplace, what are you still doing there?

## NIGHT WORK (see SHIFT WORK)

## NOISE
Noise pollution is getting worse everywhere. This damages your hearing (and hearing impairment is now the most prevalent irreversible occupational hazard in the world); it interferes with verbal

communication; it disturbs your sleep, leading to increased blood pressure, changes in respiration, cardiac arrhythmia, fatigue, and depressed mood; and it causes psychophysiological, mental health, and performance effects. Anyone who has ever lived next door to a bunch of students, a paranoid dog, or a drummer knows exactly what we mean. Cut out this entry so you can show it to your defense attorney later on.

## NORMAN, OKLAHOMA (and see CITIES)
Norman was designated "2001 Tourism Community of the Year," but you visiting tourists (both of you) might want to stick with bottled water. Norman is one of America's leading cities in terms of the degree to which its drinking water is contaminated by arsenic, which can cause cancer of the liver, bladder, lungs, kidney, and prostate.

## NOSE-BLOWING
Blowing your nose can propel mucus into your sinuses, which can make your cold worse and increase the risk of bacterial infection. Tell your date this to explain why you're letting your nose run; we're sure she'll understand.

## NOSES (see also BODY)
Noses harbor *staphylococcus aureus*, a bacterium that causes food poisoning as well as some of the most serious infections that hospital patients get. If you ask your friendly neighborhood deranged person, the one with the tinfoil hat, he will explain to you, with gestures, exactly how to protect yourself against your nose.

## NURSE, BEING A (see also DOCTOR, WORK)
And now, the less romantic side of Florence Nightingale: nurses risk exposure to blood-borne diseases including hepatitis B,

hepatitis C, AIDS, HTLV-I, HTLV-II, malaria, syphilis, babesiosis (this is when they turn into babes), brucellosis, leptospirosis, arboviral infections, relapsing fever, Creutzfeldt-Jakob disease (this is when they turn into mad cows), and viral hemorrhagic fever. They also may suffer from contact allergic dermatitis as a result of contact with latex gloves or substances such as antimicrobials, formalin, and benzocaine. You have to admit, they have a point when they say they're underpaid.

## NURSES

Well, most of them are underpaid—there are a few out there who may not deserve a raise just yet. Since 1995, at least 1,720 hospital patients have died and 9,548 others have been injured in the U.S. due to mistakes made by registered nurses.

## NURSING HOMES

There are 350,000 "adverse drug events" at nursing homes in the U.S. each year; half of these are preventable, and many are serious or life-threatening. Forty percent of nursing homes certified by the Health Care Financing Administration repeatedly failed to meet basic health and safety standards. Almost 40 percent of psychiatric services provided in nursing homes are unnecessary, lacking in psychiatric documentation, or questionable. Maybe the people running the nursing homes (and the Health Care Financing Administration) are the ones who need the psychiatric services.

## NURSING HOMES, WORKING IN (and see WORK, WORKPLACES)

Employees in nursing homes are more likely to be injured than people working in coal mines or manufacturing plants, with lost-time injury and illness rates reaching twice the U.S. average. A large proportion of these injuries could probably be prevented by teaching the employees to stop calling the patients "we" in that funny tone of voice.

## NUTS (see also FOOD, PEANUTS)

A study of cases in which children were hospitalized for choking on small objects found that nuts were the food most likely to result in injury (narrowly edging out plastic dinosaurs, VCR parts, and Mommy's earring).

## OFFICE SUPPLIES (see CORRECTION FLUID, ERASERS, PENCIL SHARPENERS, RUBBER BANDS, STAPLERS; see also WORK, WORKPLACES)

## OFFICES (see also COLLEAGUES, WORK)

Air in offices may be polluted by tobacco smoke, asbestos, formaldehyde, materials from copying machines, biological contaminants, pesticides, paints, adhesives, and vehicle exhausts from outside, leading to illnesses such as Legionnaires' disease, asthma, hypersensitivity pneumonitis, and humidifier fever, along with symptoms such as dry mucous membranes, sneezing, stuffy or runny nose, fatigue or lethargy, headache, dizziness, nausea, irritability, and forgetfulness. No wonder Dilbert and his colleagues are such a mess.

## OFF-ROAD VEHICLES (see also ALL-TERRAIN VEHICLES)

Deer mice in areas of Utah where people drive off-road vehicles are prone to infection with hantavirus, which might be transmitted to humans. If this is high on your list of things to worry about, you haven't been paying attention.

## OLD AGE

Maurice Chevalier claimed that old age isn't so bad, considering the alternative. Think again. Elderly men are more likely to get carbuncles. Elderly women are at heightened risk of conditions such as osteoporosis, incontinence, and dry eye syndrome. Elderly men and women are more susceptible to a host of conditions, including cheilosis, macular degeneration, cataracts (surgery for which has significantly less positive results with advancing age), Paget's disease, thrush, and shingles. When they become depressed, patients over sixty-five are less likely to receive effective treatment than younger patients. A study in the U.K. found that old people wait more than one-and-a-half hours longer than younger people for treatment in emergency rooms. Of course, given what happens once you finally pass from the EMERGENCY ROOM through INTENSIVE CARE into the HOSPITAL, you shouldn't be in a hurry anyway.

## OPENNESS (see also MOODS)
Newsflash: being a Rush Limbaugh fan is good for you! Having a personality that's open to learning from experience and to suggestion from others makes you more accident-prone.

## OPTIMISM (see also MOODS, PESSIMISM, SELF-ESTEEM)
Next time someone tells you, "Don't worry, be happy!" give them a swift kick. What one psychologist calls the "tyranny of the positive attitude" in America can make people feel worse and less able to cope with difficult situations.

Optimism

## ORGAN TRANSPLANTS (see also MEDICAL PROCEDURES)
People who receive organ transplants have an increased risk of getting non-Hodgkin's lymphoma, anal cancer, and ganciclovir-resistant cytomegalovirus disease. On the other hand, *not* having that transplant could bring its own problems.

## ORGASMS (and see SEX)

Believe it or not, when women's magazines run those articles telling you 101 ways to have multiple orgasms, they're not doing you any favors: research shows that orgasms can cause asthma attacks. Ninety-nine percent of women asked about this said they'd take their chances.

## OVER-THE-COUNTER DRUGS (see ACETAMINOPHEN, ASPIRIN, ALLERGY MEDICINES, ANTIHISTAMINES; see also PRESCRIPTION DRUGS)

## PACEMAKERS

If you have a pacemaker and get a staph infection, deadly pathogens can hide in the device and be impossible to detect. (So how did the researchers find out they were in there?)

## PACIFIERS (see also BABY CARE)

Pacifiers are meant to shut the kids up, right? Think again. Heavy use of pacifiers can increase the risk of ear infections among infants, and some children may be allergic to the latex of which many pacifiers are made—and we all know how quiet a sick baby can be.

### PACKAGE HOLIDAYS
#### (and see HOLIDAYS)

Cheap package holidays have been blamed for an increase in skin cancers, as more people have been able to seek the perfect tan. If you travel on a package holiday, you're more likely to get sick than people who travel independently. You're also more likely to be surrounded by perky people with too many teeth trying to get you to join in sing-alongs.

## PACKAGING

You know those packages that tell you cheerfully to "tear along the dotted line," so you fight with them for half an hour and then give up and slice them open with a knife? Doing that sends sixty thousand people a year to hospitals in the U.K.

## PAIN (and see BODY)

Suffering from widespread body pain adversely affects the immune system and kidney function, and may also mean you're more likely to die later on from cancer. Rumor has it that your local S&M club will soon be carrying Surgeon General's warnings ("THIS APPLIANCE CAN BE HAZARDOUS TO YOUR HEALTH").

## PAINTER, BEING A (and see WORK)

Painters who work with hydrocarbon solvents are at risk of developing Parkinson's disease. If only Hitler had stuck to his day job for just a little longer…

## PARENTS

As Philip Larkin says, "They f*** you up, your mum and dad." Through genetic transmission and maladroit child-raising, parents can increase their children's risk of being emotionally incompetent in dealing with the world, underachieving intellectually, being generally unhealthy, contracting lymphoma, leukemia, and cancers of the prostate, ovaries, lung, breast, thyroid, colon, or skin, and having bad eyesight. If you suffer from depression or anxiety disorders, your children are at high risk of emotional and behavioral difficulties. Children of parents suffering from post-traumatic stress disorder (PTSD) may themselves show the low cortisol levels characteristic of people with PTSD and react to trauma with extreme distress. Insecure mothers can produce toddlers with infantile anorexia. Fathers with birth defects are considerably more likely to have children with birth defects, though usually not the same as their own. Preschool children with fat or depressed mothers watch more television than other children (and if you don't understand why this is bad for you, see TELEVISION). Next time your teenaged daughter accuses you of ruining her life, keep in mind that she may have a point.

## PEACE (see also DISASTERS, RECOVERING FROM)

Suicide rates, which decrease during wartime, go back up when peace is restored. During wartime, you can probably count on someone else to do the job for you.

## PEANUTS (see also FOOD, NUTS)

If you're allergic to peanuts or peanut by-products (which are found in foods ranging from baked goods to chili and spaghetti sauces), they can give you reactions ranging from hives to ana-phylactic shock, which can cause breathing difficulties, vomit-ing, diarrhea, and even cardiac arrest. Eating peanuts contaminated by aflatoxin molds can cause liver cancer. Working for peanuts is also bad for you (see POVERTY).

## PENCIL SHARPENERS (and see OFFICE SUPPLIES)

Pencil Sharpener

Ninety-one office workers in the U.K. were injured by pencil sharpeners during the year 2000. We want to know if these were the same ninety-one who were injured by CORRECTION FLUID, and if so, what the hell they were doing on office time.

## PEOPLE

Of all the things that are bad for you, people top the list. An inter-national panel on climate change has found that most GLOBAL WARMING over the past fifty years was caused by people.

Careless treatment of the environment means that 11,046 species of plants and animals face a high risk of extinction in the near future, 180 mammal species and 182 bird species are critically endangered, freshwater wetlands have been reduced globally by up to 50 percent, soil degradation has affected two-thirds of the world's agricultural land, coastal ecosystems are losing their capacity to produce fish, and 20 to 50 percent of the world's forest cover has been destroyed. If you really want to do some good in the world, use contraception (except, of course, that CONTRACEPTIVES are bad for you…).

## PERU (see also AMERICA, CHINA, DOMINICAN REPUBLIC, EGYPT, INDIA, KENYA, MEXICO, TUNISIA)

Don't get smart on our world tour and think you can beat the odds by going somewhere off the beaten track—Peru, for example. Being original about your holiday will only make things worse. In that same study, two-thirds of the tourists who went to Peru got sick.

## PESSIMISM (see also MOODS, OPTIMISM)

If you think everything always goes wrong for you, you're probably right. Pessimists recover more slowly from heart attacks, surgery, and spinal injuries, and are more prone to severe reactions to traumatic events. They're also likely to die sooner, especially from accidents or violence. But who cares? Life sucks anyway.

## PESTICIDES (see also INSECTICIDES)

According to the World Health Organization, at least three million people are poisoned by pesticides every year, of whom more than two hundred thousand die. If you're regularly exposed to pesticides, you're more likely to experience memory loss and other cognitive dysfunctions later in life. You may be more likely to get Parkinson's disease, and if you're a man you could become infertile. Pesticides may also encourage growth of bacteria on some crops, putting you at risk if you eat raw fruit and vegetables such as strawberries and lettuce. Pesticide runoff stored in the blubber of whales is released into the females' milk, threatening the survival of some species. No, we don't know why they're still legal either, but we assume there are large amounts of money involved.

## PETS, HAVING (see also BIRDS, CATS, DOGS, DUCKLINGS; and see ANIMALS)

Asthma cases in the U.S. could drop nearly 40 percent among children under six if they didn't have allergy triggers (such as pets) in their homes. Before you auction off the Lab, though, check out the entries about CHILDREN. You might want to keep the Lab and get rid of the kid.

## PETS, NOT HAVING

People without pets have higher cholesterol and blood pressure, cope more poorly with anxiety and stress, and live less long after heart attacks. Older people without pets are less active and more likely to be depressed. And small children in homes without cats or dogs are more likely to develop eczema and hay fever. They're also more likely to get asthma—yes, we know the last entry said the opposite, but we can prove whichever theory worries you more.

## PHILADELPHIA (and see CITIES)

Among U.S. cities, Philadelphia has the third highest number of people dying as a result of pollution from power plants. It's also the third fattest city in America (looks like Philadelphia Light is a contradiction in terms).

## PHOENIX (and see CITIES, TRAFFIC)

By the time you get to Phoenix, you'll be raging. In a study of sixty-eight American cities, Phoenix was twelfth worst in terms of traffic, with almost 47 percent of daily road travel taking place in congested conditions.

## PIERCING

Body piercings can take two to nine months to heal, and nearly one in ten results in an infection, possibly even by viruses such as HIV or hepatitis B or C. "High" ear piercing can lead to perichondritis and cauliflower ear. At least one young woman is reported to have suffered an abscess of the brain following an infection in her pierced tongue. All this is unlikely to keep your teenager from getting that second stud in his eyebrow—or wherever—but you can always try.

## PILL, NOT TAKING THE

Women who don't take oral contraceptives may be more likely to develop bowel cancer. You'll have to work out the reasons for yourself.

## PILL, TAKING THE (and see CONDOMS, DIAPHRAGMS, SPERMICIDES; see also PRESCRIPTION DRUGS)

The most effective way to use the pill is to hold it between your knees: at least one in every twenty women who takes it the usual way becomes pregnant, often from taking it incorrectly. Taking the pill raises the risk of strokes and heart attacks in women over thirty-five who smoke or have high blood pressure, and women on the low-estrogen "third generation" pill have a higher risk of blood clots. Women on the pill are more likely to suffer from deep vein thrombosis as a result of long-distance air travel. The pill can alter women's sense of smell, interfering with their natural tendency to choose men whose odors signal genetic complementarity and the likelihood of healthier children. (But then, if you're on the pill, you don't want his babies anyway, so who cares?)

## PLASTICS (and see TOYS)

Some plastics used for toys, food packaging, and household products contain phthalates, chemicals that could be carcinogenic or might cause abnormalities in male sexual development. Now your son will have something else to blame you for in therapy, forty years from now.

---

### PLAYGROUNDS

If you remember childhood at all, you know that a grade-school playground is probably the most dangerous place in the universe. In 1999, more than five hundred thousand children and teenagers required medical treatment for injuries related to playground equipment, at a cost of almost $10 billion in medical, legal and liability, pain and suffering, and work loss expenses. It's unclear how many of these were actually caused by the playground equipment and how many were in the "Honest, Ms. Beasley, he just fell" category.

---

## POLLUTION

Well, if you didn't already think pollution was bad for you (for example, if you decided to back out of a worldwide treaty limiting greenhouse gases), there's a scientific probability that you may be dumber than a box of rocks. To refresh your memory as to the details, see AIR, BUSES, CARS, CITIES, POWER PLANTS, RAIN, SMOG, SPORTS UTILITY VEHICLES, TRUCKS, and WATER.

## PORTLAND, OREGON (and see CITIES, TRAFFIC)

In a study of sixty-eight American cities, Portland was ninth worst in terms of traffic, with 47 percent of daily travel taking place in congested conditions. (A lot of that traffic was the motorists passing through on their way from SAN DIEGO to SEATTLE looking for a peaceful place to drive.)

## POTTING SOIL (see also GARDENING)

People in at least three U.S. states have contracted Legionnaires' disease from handling contaminated potting soil. What we want to know is, what were you doing with legionnaires in your potting soil?

## POVERTY (see also ECONOMIC DEVELOPMENT, TOO LITTLE; MIDDLE CLASS; WEALTH)

Most of us already figured that people don't live in poverty for the good of their health, and guess what? We were right. By the age of five, poor children are already more likely than richer children to be fearful, anxious, and sad, as well as to have serious behavior problems. Poor boys are more likely to get muscular dystrophy, and both girls and boys from poor homes have a higher risk of strokes, heart disease, stomach cancer, respiratory disease, and Alzheimer's later in life. They also tend to live in places with unusually high levels of environmental toxins such as lead, polychlorinated biphenyls (PCBs), and organophosphate pesticides. If you're poor, you're more likely to suffer from fatigue; you have a higher risk of certain diseases, such as cervical or smoking-related cancers; you'll get inferior medical care for conditions such as congestive heart failure; and you're more likely to die in the weeks following a heart attack. A study in the U.K. estimated that ten thousand people, including 1,400 children, die prematurely each year because they are poor. Looks like "give me your tired, your poor" wasn't such a great offer after all. But then, we have better things to spend money on (most of which go bang or emit carbon monoxide).

## POWER LINES

If you live downwind of an electrical power line, you should sleep over at your boyfriend's more often: the lines affect particles of pollution that blow past them, you inhale the particles, and they may increase your risk of cancer.

## POWER PLANTS (and see AIR)

Nobody has ever figured out exactly what the Environmental Protection Agency does, but it doesn't appear to involve protecting the environment. Pollution from power plants cuts short the lives of over thirty thousand people in the U.S. each year, with hundreds of thousands more suffering from asthma attacks, cardiac problems, and respiratory difficulties. In 1999 alone, the 594 dirtiest power plants emitted 12.5 million tons of sulfur dioxide, 5.4 million tons of nitrogen oxide, and 2.3 billion tons of carbon dioxide.

## PREGNANCY

Sure, you were prepared for morning sickness, backache, stretch marks, and the rest of it, but we bet nobody warned you about drawbacks like these: getting pregnant increases the likelihood that a woman will become obsessive-compulsive, die of homicide, suffer from deep vein thrombosis when flying long distances, or come down with malaria.

## PRESCRIPTION DRUGS (see also ANTIBIOTICS, ANTIDEPRESSANTS, BETA-BLOCKERS, CANCER DRUGS, DRUG TRIALS, EPILEPSY DRUGS, ESTROGEN, HORMONE REPLACEMENT THERAPY, PILL; and see DOCTORS, MEDICAL DIAGNOSES, OVER-THE-COUNTER DRUGS)

Every year, 1.5 million Americans have to be hospitalized due to adverse drug reactions, which can cause depression, hallucinations or psychoses, sexual dysfunction, dementia, falls and hip fractures, and automobile accidents; and seven thousand die as a result of "medication errors." "Prescribing errors" by doctors are often at fault: over a fourteen-year period, one medical center documented 20,966 such errors, notably involving antimicrobials, cardiovascular agents, gastrointestinal agents, analgesics, and hormonal agents. And this is your brain on *prescription* drugs...

## PRIEST, BEING A
A study in the U.K. found that priests in the Church of England are abused, assaulted, or murdered at rates only matched by police officers. Evidence suggests that the people who do the automated voices you get when you phone the electric company would be at the top of the list, if only we could get at them.

### PRINTER, BEING A (and see WORK)
Printers often work with hydrocarbon solvents, so they're at heightened risk of developing Parkinson's disease. Back when type had to be set by hand, this led to a lot of interesting headlines.

### PROSTITUTE, BEING A (and see WORK)
A study in the U.K. found that half of prostitutes working outdoors and more than one-fourth of those working indoors had suffered violence from clients in the previous six months. Gee, we always thought they went into the business because you get to meet such great people.

### PSYCHIATRIST, BEING A (and see WORK)
A study in the U.K. found that nearly 20 percent of psychiatrists had been assaulted by their patients in the previous year. Somehow, it's hard to get too surprised about this.

## PUBLIC RELATIONS SPECIALIST, BEING A (and see WORK)

Public relations specialists have an unusually high risk of dying from asthma. And we thought we were the only ones who choked on the things they said.

## PUMPKINS (see also FOOD)

Here's one for the Weird Statistics file: smokers who eat pumpkin increase their risk of lung cancer. Happy Thanksgiving!

## RACE

You won't be surprised to hear this by now, but your ethnic background is bad for you—no matter what it is. If you're white, for example, you're much more likely than African Americans to die while being treated in Veterans Affairs hospitals, or to get osteoporosis and bladder cancer or melanoma, as well as to commit suicide (if you're a white male) and to recover less well mentally from coronary artery disease. If you're African American, on the other hand, you're at much greater risk than whites of contracting or dying from breast and other cancers, hypertension, diabetes, childhood asthma, or (if you're a woman) fatal complications in pregnancy, as well as receiving inferior medical treatment for conditions ranging from glaucoma to heart attacks. Hispanics are 20 percent more likely than blacks or whites to die from injuries at work, 50 percent more likely than whites to die of diabetes, and only half as likely to have a high school education; they receive worse care when they get AIDS, and are at greater risk of having undiagnosed glaucoma. Native Americans have a higher incidence of smoking and of driving without seat belts, as well as having limited access to health care and suffering disproportionately from poor health, obesity, lack of exercise, and diabetes, which afflicts the Pima Indians in Arizona more than any other group in the world. Asian Americans have the highest rate of late HIV intervention of any ethnic group, are three to five times as likely as whites to get liver cancer, are five times as likely (at least in the case of Vietnamese women) to get cervical cancer, and die of heart attacks in unusual numbers on the fourth day of each month, stressed by the fact that the words for "four" and "death" are linguistically very similar in Mandarin, Cantonese, and Japanese. The only good news is that if you're Asian American, this is your kind of book: you're more likely than whites to be pessimistic about life.

## RAIN

If you thought you could escape the perils of the SUN by living somewhere nice and rainy, you were wrong. More than 20 million tons of sulfur dioxide and nitrogen oxides are poured into the atmosphere each year as a result of burning fossil fuels; a large proportion of these compounds returns to the earth in the form of acid

Rain

rain, which injures trees, kills off fish in lakes and streams, damages buildings, reduces visibility, and produces lung disorders such as asthma and bronchitis. (We were going to put this information in an entry called FOSSIL FUELS, but then this very large man with steel-toed Doc Martens and a Henry Ford T-shirt showed up at our door and explained in small words and big gestures why that would be a bad idea. So we put it under RAIN and he gave us a nice new Focus LX.)

## REFEREE, BEING A (and see WORK)

In the past decade, hundreds of referees and other sports officials have been physically assaulted, or have had their cars vandalized or their pets attacked, by players, coaches, and fans upset about their decisions during games. Yelling insults about the ref's mother is one thing, but you have to worry about any fan who has enough dedication to find out where his hamster lives.

## REFRIGERATORS, EMPTY

Elderly people with empty refrigerators are more likely to be admitted to hospitals than elderly people whose refrigerators are not empty. Remember, somebody paid for this study. You or I could have told them for free that people who can't afford food are more likely to get sick, and then they could have used the funding to fill up those refrigerators.

## REFUGEE, BEING A

Another one for the "duh" file: refugees have a higher than normal incidence of tuberculosis, hepatitis B, intestinal parasites, nutritional deficiencies, and depression.

## RENTER, BEING A

If you're renting your home, you're 50 percent more likely to be a victim of property crimes than people who own the place where they live. (The criminals can't be all that bright, considering that people who can afford to own houses probably have a lot more stuff worth stealing.)

## RESPIRATORY INFECTIONS (see also DISEASES)

For the One-Damn-Thing-After-Another file: having a chronic respiratory infection can lead to atherosclerosis, heart attacks, and strokes.

## RESPIRATORY THERAPIST, BEING A (and see WORK)

Irony of the Day: respiratory therapists have an unusually high risk of dying from asthma.

## RICE (see also FOOD)

Rice paddies emit significant quantities of the hydrocarbons that result in global warming and damage to the ozone layer. Of course, this entry must be imaginary anyway, since GLOBAL WARMING is a myth. So don't worry.

## RICHMOND (and see CITIES)

Over a ten-year period, Richmond, Virginia, was described as having the fourth highest murder rate in the U.S., two-and-a-half times the average for major American cities. If you have ever read anything by Patricia Cornwell, this won't surprise you one little bit.

## RING FINGERS, SHORT (and see BODY)

Men whose ring fingers are the same length as or shorter than their index fingers have a greatly increased risk of heart attacks in their thirties and forties. Sawing off the ends of your index fingers is not the answer, but we like the way you think.

## RUBBER BANDS (and see OFFICE SUPPLIES)

Rubber bands injured 402 office workers in the U.K. during the year 2000. We leave the rest to your imagination.

## RUGS (see CARPETS)

## RUNNING (see also SPORTS)

If you run marathons, you could develop breathing difficulties such as asthma or tightening of the airways in the presence of pollen or cold weather, along with changes in blood chemistry that could give you heart attacks. Find a nice safe sport instead, like Formula One racing.

## RURAL AREAS (see also CITIES)

The more remote the rural area in which you live, the more likely you are to suffer from premature Limiting Long-Term Illness (no, we don't know what it is either).

## SALT (see also FOOD)

We all know that too much salt can raise your blood pressure, but that's not all: it might give you stomach cancer as well. On the other hand, when you read the labels on most processed foods, the two main ingredients appear to be "salt" and "reconstituted cardboard" (you think we're kidding, right?); imagine what they'd taste like without the salt.

## SAN DIEGO (and see CITIES, TRAFFIC)

In a study of sixty-eight American cities, San Diego ranked eighth in terms of the amount of daily road travel that takes place in congested conditions. Time to head north?

## SAN FRANCISCO (and see CITIES, TRAFFIC)

Wrong—moving up the West Coast won't do you any good at all. San Francisco was second worst in terms of traffic, with almost half of travel taking place in congested conditions. Think you might do better heading on to SEATTLE?

## SAND

Workers in the industrial sand industry risk kidney disease as a result of exposure to silica. Your neighborhood sandbox is probably fairly safe, though, if you could only convince the woman next door that her toddler really does still need his diapers.

## SCHOOLS (see also HIGH SCHOOLS)

If your kid claims he's allergic to school, he may actually be right. Two million children are allergic to foods served in school cafeterias—including milk, eggs, peanuts, wheat, soy, and fish—and many others suffer asthma and allergy attacks due to substances found in classrooms, including chalk dust, dust mites, animal dander from class pets or pet hair on other students' clothing, pollen, and mold. And don't count on their allergy medicine to solve the problem: in a recent study, half of school nurses reported errors in providing medications to students in their schools over the previous year. (As far as we could tell from their responses—"*Duuuude!*"—the students didn't have any problem with this.)

## SCHOOLS, SECURITY MEASURES IN

Security measures in schools may make students feel less secure. They could also be a threat to students' rights through introduction of surveillance cameras, backpack searches, drug tests, dress codes, and restrictions on language. We're not in Norman Rockwell country anymore, Toto....

## SCHOOLMATES

Three high school boys in five said they could get a gun if they wanted to, and one boy in five said he had taken a weapon to school during the year before a recent study. But then, five out of five high school boys will say just about anything they think makes them sound macho, so go figure.

## SCOOTERS

Accidents involving foot-propelled scooters are increasing rapidly: more than seven thousand people per month (one-fourth of whom were less than eight years old) required emergency-room care after such accidents toward the end of 2000. You have to wonder about the other three-fourths.

Scooter

## SCUBA DIVING (see also SPORTS)

Scuba diving can quintuple your risk of ischaemic brain lesions. No, we've never heard of them either, so we figure the risk can't have been too high to start with. Hang on to the wet suit.

## SEA, SWIMMING IN THE

If you're swimming in the sea, you have one chance in twenty of becoming ill from sewage contamination even when the water quality has been defined as "acceptable." (The Environmental Protection Agency Dictionary defines "acceptable" as "adj. We threw a match in the water and it didn't catch fire.")

## SEAFOOD, EATING (and see FOOD)

Of all the things people eat, seafood is most likely to cause food-poisoning outbreaks. Shellfish contaminated by sewage kill twenty-five thousand people each year and cause 2.5 million cases of hepatitis. In addition, methylmercury in seafood may cause neurological problems in as many as sixty thousand children annually, leading to recommendations by various groups that pregnant women avoid eating swordfish, king mackerel, shark, tilefish, tuna steaks, sea bass, oysters from the Gulf of Mexico, marlin, halibut, pike, walleye, white croaker, and large-mouth bass. Remember how, way back when, they used to call it "brain food"?

## SEAFOOD, NOT EATING

Men on a fish-free diet are two to three times more likely to get prostate cancer than men who eat lots of fatty fish such as salmon, mackerel, and herring. Pregnant women who eat too little fish are more likely to have premature babies (but then, see SEAFOOD, EATING; by the time you find a fish that isn't a major source of methylmercury, the kid will be in college anyway). A study has found that people who eat fish less than once a week run a 31 percent higher risk of mild to severe depression than people who eat it more often. Older adults who don't eat fatty fish each week are more likely to die of heart attacks. If you're a smoker, not eating lots of fresh fish means you're more likely to get lung cancer—but then, that obviously doesn't bother you too much.

## SEATTLE (and see CITIES, TRAFFIC)

If you've been heading up the West Coast from SAN DIEGO in search of a peaceful drive to work, forget it: in that study of American cities, Seattle was fifth worst in terms of traffic, with almost half of travel taking place in congested conditions.

## SELF-ESTEEM (see also MOODS, OPTIMISM)

Recent studies suggest that the higher your self-esteem, the more likely you are to be a threat to the people around you. (If you watch *Jerry Springer*, you already knew this.)

## SEX (and see HERPES, ORGASMS)

Way back when your Sunday school teacher and your mother told you never to do the nasty, they had a point. We've got a list of sexually transmitted diseases as long as your...whatever: AIDS, hepatitis B, human papillomaviruses (which cause genital warts and cancer), chlamydia, trichomoniasis, syphilis, gonorrhea, pediculosis, and many more. A lot of these can kill you— and the rest make you wish you were dead. Plus, men who have a large number of sexual partners have a higher risk of prostate cancer. (We're sure this news will change your life forever. Britney: Yes! Yes! Take me now, you big stud rhino! You: No, honey, I don't want to get prostate cancer in forty years, let's just cuddle.) Oh, and sex can also lead to dehydration, though that's the least of your problems.

## SEX, ONLINE

If you're addicted to cybersex (there are about two hundred thousand of you out there in the U.S. alone, and you know who you are), you may end up locking yourself away with your modem for hours at a time, lingering online at the office, forgetting to do the dishes or pick up your children at school, losing interest in normal sexual activities, becoming withdrawn and brooding, and then hiding your credit card bills and lying about your reasons for using the Internet. If you move it offline and hook up with HotLilMuffin or SagittarianStud for a quickie, you're more likely to get sexually transmitted diseases than if you make your contacts in other ways.

## SEX, ORAL

Whatever Debbie back in seventh grade told you, you can't get pregnant through oral sex; you can, however, get AIDS and other unpleasant diseases. More and more teenagers are having oral sex, and this has led to reports of dramatic increases in oral herpes and gonorrhea of the pharynx. In extreme cases, oral sex can cause months of Senate hearings and endless bad jokes about blue cocktail dresses.

## SHAMPOOING

According to the British Stroke Association, people have suffered strokes while bending their heads over basins to have their hair washed by hairdressers. (And that's nothing compared with what's happening to the HAIRDRESSER.) Is no place safe?

## SHIFT WORK (and see SLEEP, WORK, WORKPLACES)

Working night shifts may give you peptic ulcers, breast cancer, and heart and blood pressure problems. It may also make you less alert and more accident-prone, and these effects get worse when workers rotate shifts rather than sticking to a late-night routine. This should reassure you everywhere from the ER (where it's been found that surgeons make more mistakes after long night shifts) to the night train.

## SHOPPING CARTS

We all know shopping carts have minds of their own, but every now and then they can turn vicious. More than twenty thousand children under six are treated in hospital emergency rooms in the U.S. each year for shopping-cart injuries. The shopping carts involved are painlessly put to sleep.

---

### SHORT, BEING
#### (see also LEGS, SHORT; and TALL)

Short children are at increased risk of high blood pressure in later life. Short men receive poorer educations (this may be because they spend half their schooldays being dangled over the banisters or shut into someone's locker), and are less likely to marry and have children (it's hard to impress girls when everybody calls you "Squirt"). Short people are more likely to get Alzheimer's (which is probably a blessing: who wants to remember that kind of life?). To add insult to injury, there's that Randy Newman song about how you have no reason to live.

---

## SHYNESS (see also MOODS)

Shy schoolchildren do less well on tests; they can't get up the courage to ask the kid next to them for the answers.

## SINGLE, BEING (see UNMARRIED)

## SITTING

Buddhists and other meditators take note: sitting for long periods without changing position is a risk factor for lower back disorders. If you reach an advanced enough state of mindfulness, you may be able to transcend the pain, but no studies have been done on this so far. (We have applied for government funding and will be keeping you updated. Meanwhile, keep meditating.)

## SKATING, IN-LINE

In-line skating injuries, 40 percent of which involve fractures or dislocations and 5 percent of which involve head injuries, cost almost $350 million annually for emergency-room visits alone. Always skate out of line.

### SKIING (see also SPORTS)

Skiers suffer from knee conditions such as chondromalacia. Cross-country skiers are at risk of developing breathing problems such as spasms of the airways. We haven't seen any studies on what those tight pants do to you, but we can guess.

## SKIN CARE

If you're pregnant, you could damage your unborn child's health by using skin care products, including some herbal remedies, that are intended for purposes such as treating acne, promoting hair growth, or healing fungal conditions. Your baby's better off with a spotty, bald, moldy mother.

### SLEDDING (see also SPORTS)

Sledding accidents, two-thirds of which are sustained by youths aged fourteen and under, result in medical, legal, and insurance costs of more than $350 million annually. Help the economy— buy your kid a sled.

## SLEEP, TOO LITTLE (see also FATIGUE, SHIFT WORK)

A lack of sleep—and is there *anyone* out there who's getting enough sleep?—interferes with your body's ability to metabolize carbohydrates. This can increase the severity of diabetes, high blood pressure, and obesity. Staying awake for as little as seventeen to nineteen hours can reduce your physical and mental reaction times as much as two alcoholic drinks (and is a lot less fun); and regularly sleeping less than four hours a night significantly increases your death rate. In younger people, lack of sleep can lead to behavior problems, increased use of stimulants, poor performance in school, and greater risk of injury and death, especially in auto accidents. In older people, problems with sleeping can be followed by depression. Inadequate sleep can also cause premature aging. Photocopy this page for your boss next time he asks you to come to work early.

## SLEEP, TOO MUCH

And for the tiny percentage of you who get plenty of sleep: don't get too pleased with yourselves. Sleeping eight or more hours a night increases your risk of strokes and an early death. Excessive sleepiness, particularly in the daytime, may reflect hypersomnia or narcolepsy, a condition that can involve sudden losses of muscle tone, sleep paralysis, hypnagogic hallucinations, and lapses of memory.

## SLEEPING ON ONE SIDE

Habitually sleeping on one side may make the kidney on the weight-bearing side more likely to develop stones. Rumor has it that this may have been the way Isaac Newton really discovered gravity.

## SLUDGE

Sewage sludge that has been converted to fertilizer (and what else can you do with sewage sludge?) can transmit E. coli, salmonella, hepatitis B, and other bacteria and viruses.

### SMOG (and see AIR)

No surprises here: smog is a health problem, no matter how hard the auto companies try to say it isn't (from the Official Auto Company Dictionary: "smog, n. What smog?"). Smog results in fifty-three thousand hospitalizations, sends 159,000 people to emergency rooms, and triggers 6.2 million asthma attacks each summer in the eastern half of the United States.

## SMOG, REDUCING

Don't think cutting down on smog is the answer, though. Smog absorbs the sun's heat and masks the effects of global warming. When clean air laws reduce the amount of smog in the air, global warming becomes more evident. There's also more SUN.

## SMOKERS

It makes a lot of sense to keep the smokers in the car park (or on some other continent, a strategy the tobacco companies are now working on). A woman exposed to others' cigarette smoke may have difficulty becoming pregnant. If you do get pregnant and are exposed to smoke, you're more likely to give birth to a baby that is underweight and suffers from loss of lung function at least through its teens. Infants in smokers' households are more likely to die, and children will be at risk from respiratory diseases and ear infections. Adult women exposed to smokers double their risk of heart attacks, and environmental tobacco smoke has been associated with adult-onset asthma. Still, how much difference would it make to the quality of your air if we got rid of all the smokers and kept the CARS?

# SMOKING

Guess what? The Surgeon General is right: smoking's not good for you. Smoking impairs the health of your muscles, bones, and joints, increases your risk of being injured when you exercise (the usual smoker's solution: so don't exercise), causes loss of bone mass, significantly slows the healing of fractures, and makes it more

Smoking

likely that you'll lose your teeth. It also causes 60 percent of fatal cancers that affect smokers, notably cancers of the lungs (lung cancer death rates among American women went up by 600 percent between 1950 and 2000), mouth, throat, esophagus, bladder, breast, skin, pancreas, and anus; it leads to heart disease (30 percent of all U.S. deaths from heart disease are a result of smoking), emphysema, and perforated peptic ulcers, causes ruptured aneurisms, rheumatoid arthritis, hearing impairment, and impotence, increases women's risk of undergoing delays in conceiving, becoming infertile, or developing multiple sclerosis, and quadruples the likelihood of life-threatening blood infections or meningitis from *Streptococcus pneumoniae*. If you smoke while pregnant, you're much more likely to have children who have behavior problems and are at risk of drug addiction later in life. Smoking is strongly associated with mental illness in the population as a whole, and with depression and anxiety disorders in teenagers. Adolescents who fight, drive while drunk, and generally take risks are more likely to be smokers. People who smoke are less likely to benefit from balloon angioplasty and other procedures to open obstructed heart arteries. Smoking results in 430,000 deaths a year in the U.S.; by 2020 it may cause more deaths in most developing countries than AIDS, malaria, tuberculosis, automobile crashes, homicides, and suicides combined; and by 2030 it is expected to be the single biggest cause of death worldwide. Smoking is also a leading cause of fires and death from fires. It also greatly increases your risk of getting long lectures from complete strangers about how you're polluting the air. (The only way to get rid of these helpful people is to ask them if they drive CARS. They always do.) Before you non-smokers get too pleased with yourselves, see "SMOKING, NOT."

## SMOKING, CUTTING BACK ON (see also CIGARETTES, LOW-TAR)

If you're cutting down on cigarettes, don't bother. People absorb just as many toxins from their cigarettes when they cut their smoking in half, since they smoke their remaining cigarettes twice as hard. On the other hand, they only get half as many lectures about air pollution from those helpful strangers in their SUVs.

## SMOKING, NOT

Non-smokers have higher rates of Parkinson's disease than people who smoke. Before you light up in panic, however, take another look at "SMOKING."

## SMOKING, QUITTING

People who quit smoking have a heightened risk of major depression. Quitting smoking also imposes serious fiscal strains on governments, whose costs for health care and pensions increase as people live longer. If you're an anarchist, quit now.

## SMOKING WHILE SUNBATHING

It's official: smoking definitely does not make you look cool. In fact, it breaks down the connective tissue that maintains the skin's elasticity, which can combine with exposure to sunlight to make you look much older. Being too concerned about this is ageism, of course, but you still might want to keep it in mind.

## SNORING

Very loud snoring interrupted by intermittent pauses in breathing may be a sign of obstructive sleep apnea. This can make normal sleep impossible, lead to severe daytime fatigue and irritability, cause headaches, reduce interest in sex, increase the risk of auto accidents by three to five times, and result in heart disease and strokes—and that's just in the snorer, not in the lucky person sharing his or her bed.

## SNOWBOARDING (see also SPORTS)

Snowboarding accidents can lead to injuries of the wrist, shoulder, head, face, chest, abdomen, and spine. If global warming does exist, though, you won't have to worry about this for long.

## SOAP (and see CLEANLINESS, DIRTINESS)

Half of all hand soaps contain antibacterials. They brag about this in the ads, but what they don't tell you is that antibacterials can promote the emergence of bacteria that are resistant to antibiotics. ("Gee, honey! Let's buy the soap that means our grandchildren will die of diseases that haven't killed anyone outside the Third World in fifty years!")

## SOCCER, PLAYING (see also SPORTS)

Through heading the ball or suffering concussions, soccer players are at risk of chronic traumatic brain injury, leading to impaired performance in memory and planning functions. (In some soccer players it can be hard to tell the difference, but scientists use special equipment.) Soccer players also suffer from knee conditions such as chondromalacia, and can suffer later in life from osteoarthritis.

## SOFTBALL BATS

And our final nomination for the Elvis Award for Least Dignified Way to Die: in May 1999, forty-five thousand softball bats were recalled when the tops began to shear off, posing a danger of injury to batters and bystanders.

### SOFT DRINKS
#### (see also DRINKS)

Active teenage girls who drink carbonated beverages are much more likely to break bones. Consumption of soft drinks is also associated with obesity, tooth decay, heart disease, kidney stones, caffeine addiction, and the risk of osteoporosis later in life, and the caffeine in some soft drinks can increase the risk of miscarriages. (These studies took a while, because they had to go to an isolated island off Papua New Guinea to find a control group.)

## SOOT

Looks like Mary Poppins was wrong: a sweep *isn't* as lucky as lucky can be. Soot has been linked to cancer, respiratory illness, and the premature death of fifty thousand people from illness each year, as well as being responsible for 15 to 30 percent of global warming.

## SORE THROATS (see also DISEASES)

Strep throats in children can cause obsessive-compulsive or tic disorders. The real problem here is that, with little kids, when one kid catches something, so does the whole class...

## SOUTH, THE (see also ARKANSAS, LOUISIANA, MISSISSIPPI, SOUTH CAROLINA, WEST VIRGINIA)

People who live in some southern states are more likely to pay high health insurance premiums or have no health insurance; they suffer from excessive rates of disease and receive poor-quality medical care. Women in the rural South have a particularly great risk of death from heart disease, especially in the lower Mississippi Valley—heart disease experts call it Coronary Valley. People in the South are most likely to die of strokes after release from hospital. Plus, global warming is going to cause rising sea levels and storm surges, which will threaten human coastal development and natural ecosystems. Before you start packing, though, check out the other options (EAST, MIDWEST, WEST).

## SOUTH CAROLINA (and see STATES)

South Carolina is the third most unhealthy state in the U.S. On the other hand, the odds are pretty good you don't live there anyway.

## SOYA BEANS (see also FOOD)

If you eat a diet high in soya beans while you're pregnant, your child may suffer long-term developmental damage. (So how has Japan made it this far?)

## SPERMICIDES

Women who use a common spermicide may increase their risk of contracting HIV from an HIV-positive partner. DIAPHRAGMS and the PILL aren't likely to help, and asking your partner to use a CONDOM has risks of its own. We warned you there was no such thing as safe sex.

## SPORTS, PLAYING (see also ATHLETE, BASEBALL, BASKETBALL, DIVING, FOOTBALL, GOLF, GYMNASTICS, HOCKEY, HORSEBACK RIDING, JOGGING, RUNNING, SCUBA DIVING, SKIING, SLEDDING, SNOWBOARDING, SOCCER, SWIMMING, TENNIS, TRAMPOLINES, WRESTLING)

All you couch potatoes, give yourselves a pat on the back (if you can reach that far): as a health measure, playing sports is over-rated. More than eighty thousand people annually suffer brain injuries during recreational sports, or at least sports that were supposed to be recreational. And more than 775,000 children under the age of fifteen are treated in hospital emergency rooms in the United States each year for sports injuries ranging from bruises and sprains to fractures and severe injuries to the neck and spinal cord.

## SPORTS, WATCHING

If you're desperate to drag him away from the playoffs, here's your leverage: watching important sporting events can cause deaths among men from heart attacks and strokes.

## SPORTS UTILITY VEHICLES (see also AIR, CARS)

No matter what you may think, you and your SUV are not cool. If you own an SUV, your vehicle is much more likely to roll over, leaving your overall chances of being killed in an accident the same as for occupants of ordinary cars; and if you collide with someone else, they're three times more likely to be killed than if you'd been driving an ordinary car. The greater dangers associated with SUVs mean you'll pay higher insurance premiums. Large SUVs get extremely poor gas mileage, and—for some reason that could not possibly have anything to do with the political clout of the auto and oil industries—they are allowed to release several times as much smog-causing pollution as cars. Remind us: why exactly did you buy the damn thing in the first place?

## SPRING (see also SUMMER, AUTUMN, WINTER)

The joys of spring are clearly overrated. Spring is the peak time for suicides in the United States. People born in the spring live four to seven months less long than people born in the fall. And late spring is high season for strokes.

## ST. JOHN'S WORT, TAKING (see also ANTIDEPRESSANTS, HERBAL REMEDIES)

The alternative antidepressant St. John's wort can interfere with some prescription medicines, including birth control pills, antibiotics, AIDS treatments, cardiac drugs, and anti-rejection drugs taken by transplant patients, and it can have adverse effects on pregnancy and prolong the sedative effects of anesthesia following surgery. It also may not work—well, in fairness, very few antidepressants work if your birth control pills, antibiotics, and heart medicine have all let you down.

## ST. JOHN'S WORT, STOPPING TAKING

Doctors may have to increase your dosage of prescription drugs if you're taking St. John's wort, because it can reduce the levels of the drugs in your blood. If you then stop taking the wort, your blood levels of the drugs can increase dangerously. (Of course, in that case, it's actually the prescription drug that's bad for you, but the study wasn't about to point this out.)

## ST. LOUIS (and see CITIES)

Over a ten-year period, St. Louis had the fifth highest murder rate in the U.S., more than two-and-a-half times the average for major American cities. On the other hand, they have the world's only set of three-foot-high fiberglass teeth (no, really), so don't cancel your holiday bookings just yet.

### STAPLERS (and see OFFICE SUPPLIES)

Stapler

In the U.K. alone, 1,317 office workers were injured by staples and staplers during the year 2000. There are times when the question "I wonder what would happen if I..." is better left unanswered.

### STATES (see ARKANSAS, LOUISIANA, MISSISSIPPI, NEVADA, SOUTH CAROLINA, WEST VIRGINIA)

### STRESS (and see WORK)

Stress can take away your appetite, suppress your immune system, squash your sex drive, make you infertile and irritable, and give you panic attacks, depression, diabetes, and hypertension. It can make vaccines less effective, give you asthma, diseases of the gastrointestinal tract, memory loss, and back pain, and weaken your skin's ability to heal wounds and fight disease. If you're under stress around the time you get pregnant, your baby may have an increased risk of congenital defects such as heart problems, neural tube defects, or cleft lips; if you're stressed during pregnancy, the child may risk a heart attack later in life. HIV-positive people under stress progress more rapidly to AIDS. Maybe we should have warned you about this at the beginning of this book.

### STROLLERS (see also BABY CARE)

In 1999, 12,600 children under the age of five were injured in falls from strollers and baby carriages. Like we said, leave the kid at home.

### STUPIDITY (see INTELLIGENCE, LOW)

### SUMMER (see also AUTUMN, WINTER, SPRING)

Summertime, and the living ain't as easy as you think. People born in the summer have a higher risk of eating disorders, depression, and dyslexia, and are more likely to kill themselves when they get old and less likely than children born in the fall to grow up to be star soccer players (which is actually not such a bad thing; see SOCCER). Summer also brings an upsurge in diseases spread by ticks or mosquitoes such as West Nile virus, dengue fever, Lyme disease, babesiosis, and ehrlichiosis. With greater air pollution and earlier summers, more people suffer from hay fever, which causes congestion, sneezing, itching, and runny nose, and leads in some cases to asthma or even death from pneumonia, chronic obstructive pulmonary disease, or heart attacks. Hot weather can lead to depression, irritability, and violence—so if you're in air conditioning sales, watch out next time you tell that desperate client you might get around to him in November.

## SUN, TOO LITTLE

Too little exposure to sunlight may result in vitamin D deficiency, a condition that can cause the painful bone disease osteomalacia, as well as exacerbate bone loss, osteoporosis, and the risk of fractures, especially in adults over fifty. A lack of vitamin D is also causing rickets in increasing numbers of children. Too little sun can give you prostate cancer or seasonal affective disorder (SAD), whose symptoms include depression, lethargy, and an inability to concentrate, along with overeating and weight gain. No wonder the Vikings decided to leave Denmark (we're only surprised they managed to drag themselves out of bed).

## SUN, TOO MUCH (see also MOON)

Maybe the Vikings should have stayed in Denmark. Too much exposure to sun can result in basal-cell carcinomas, melanoma (the most serious form of skin cancer), other cancers (as a result of gene damage and impairment of the workings of the immune system), and premature aging of the skin, or photoaging. Excessive exposure to sunlight in early life can lead later on to age-related maculopathy, a deterioration of the retina of the eye that is the leading cause of irreversible visual loss in the industrialized world.

## SUNBEDS

From the Hollywood Book of Really Tough Logic Puzzles: if too much exposure to the sun gives you skin cancer, what might you get from too much time on sunbeds whose tanning lamps mimic the effects of sunshine? If you answered, "Double the risk of developing squamous cell and basal cell carcinomas," give yourself five points. If you answered, "A totally cool tan," give yourself health insurance.

## SUNGLASSES

Celebrities take note: wearing sunglasses with colored lenses can affect your vision or make you color-blind.

## SUNSCREEN

Like we said, one of the few things we all still believe in (along with EXERCISE and drinking lots of WATER) is sunscreen—and we're sorry to tell you this, but even sunscreen is overrated. It protects you against the ultraviolet B radiation that leads to sunburn, but it only partly screens ultraviolet A rays, which produce fatal melanomas. Getting too confident about the effectiveness of sunscreen leads people to spend too much time in the sun; as a result, according to some studies, the more you use sunscreen, the more likely you are to get melanomas. In addition, a chemical used in most sunscreens may damage human cells. Has your crisis of faith kicked in yet?

## SUPER BOWL

If you and your spouse both want to watch the Super Bowl, that's great—just do it in different places. Super Bowl Sunday is the worst day of the year for domestic violence in the U.S.

### SWEETS (see also FOOD)

Eating a lot of sweets increases your risk of developing cancer of the colon. Explaining this to your toddler when he screams for candy at the checkout will not work.

### SWIMMING (see also SEA, SPORTS)

Some researchers theorize that by-products of the chlorine in indoor swimming pools could cause pregnant women to mis-carry or lead to birth defects in their children. Competitive swim-mers run a heightened risk of developing breathing problems such as asthma. And swimmers' hair may turn green because of copper ions in the water. (Of course, in some subcultures, that adds a lot to your street cred.)

### SWIMMING LESSONS

Swimming lessons for children under four can give them and their parents a false sense of security without making it safer for them to be around water, possibly leading to an increased risk of drowning. Basically, feeling too safe is bad for you; but now you have this book, you'll never have to worry about that again!

### TALL, BEING (see also MOTHERS, TALL; and SHORT)

Tall women are more likely than short women to fracture their hips (they have farther to fall) and to develop breast cancer.

## TATTOOS

People being tattooed risk allergic responses to the pigments, as well as exposure to blood-borne pathogens. Many potential blood donors have to be disqualified because they have been tattooed during the previous year. Next time a three-hundred-pound Hell's Angel covered in prison tattoos sits next to you on the bus, explain this to him. We're sure he'll see the error of his ways.

## TAXICAB DRIVER, BEING A (and see WORK)

Taxicab

Driving a taxicab is the occupation in which you are most likely to be murdered. (If you've ever been in one of those taxis where the driver speaks no known language and clearly arrived in the city about three hours ago, you'll understand this.) Taxicab drivers also have an unusually high rate of deaths from pulmonary tuberculosis.

## TEA, DRINKING (see also COFFEE, DRINKS)

The caffeine in tea can increase the risk of miscarriages. Rumor has it that pro-life groups are campaigning to make tea illegal.

## TEA, NOT DRINKING

Older men who don't consume catechins, a type of flavonoid found in black tea, are more likely to die from heart disease. When possession of tea becomes a Class A felony, you guys are in real trouble.

## TEETH, GRINDING (see also GUM DISEASE; and see BODY)

If you grind your teeth in your sleep, you're likely to suffer from anxiety, joint discomfort and muscle aches, premature loss of teeth, sleep disruption, daytime sleepiness, and headaches—although these last three may be because your bedmate is smacking you across the back of the head to try and make you knock it off.

## TEFLON

According to one report, Teflon used in cookware, insulation, fibers, and motor oils releases chemicals into the environment that take centuries to break down and whose long-term effects are unknown. Isn't it nice to know we may be leaving something for our great-grandkids to remember us by?

## TELEVISION (see also COMPUTER GAMES, MOVIES, VIDEO GAMES)

More than one thousand studies show a causal relationship between violence in media, including television, and aggressive behavior in children, with measurable and long-lasting effects including emotional desensitization toward violence in real life. (Nobody has yet proved that Tom and Jerry are directly responsible for a recent series of gruesome murders involving a giant hammer and a talking bulldog, but we'll leave you to draw your own conclusions.) Grade-school children can develop eating disorders and stereotyped views of ideal body size as a result of watching television—unsurprisingly, as your average female TV star appears to be twenty or thirty pounds lighter than your average grade-school child. Children who watch the most television are most likely to pester their parents for toys and presents— which we suppose may not actually be bad for you, if you have unlimited amounts of money and closet space. Alzheimer's patients tend to have watched more than average amounts of television in their younger years, and men who watch lots of television have a significantly increased risk of diabetes. Turn it off and go get a life.

## TELEVISION NEWS

Forget bringing up your kids to be socially aware. Children exposed to vivid news coverage of violence could suffer from post-traumatic stress syndrome and other problems.

## TENNIS (see also SPORTS)

Tennis players have a high risk of skin cancers because of their extensive exposure to the sun. The referees are the ones in real trouble: they not only get exposed to the sun, they also get exposed to the tennis players.

## TEXTILE WORKER, BEING A (and see WORK)

Here's something new for you to feel guilty about: wearing clothes. Textile workers have an unusually high incidence of chronic obstructive pulmonary disease and byssinosis.

## THANKSGIVING (see PUMPKINS, TURKEY, and HOLIDAYS)

## THIN, BEING TOO (see also EATING TOO LITTLE, FAT)

If your body is more Homer Simpson than heroically slim, here's the silver lining: being thinner would mean you'd be at greater risk of getting Alzheimer's disease. Men who are seriously underweight are also 77 percent more likely than men of average weight to try suicide, and 25 percent more likely to be seriously depressed.

## THRIFT STORES (see also WORKPLACES)

Two-thirds of thrift stores in the U.S. sell items considered hazardous by the U.S. Consumer Product Safety Commission. Examples: unsafe drawstrings on children's outerwear, hair dryers without protection against electrocution, cribs that don't meet current safety standards, and recalled infant car seat carriers. Yet another reason not to be poor (or thrifty).

## TIGER WOODS (and see GOLF)

Erratic golfers struggling to emulate the power of Tiger Woods's drives have injured spectators or themselves, leading to numerous lawsuits. No matter how you feel as you're standing at the tee, remember, you are *not* Tiger Woods. (Tiger, this doesn't count you.)

## TOYS (see also BABY CARE)
More than seventy thousand children under five were treated in hospital emergency rooms during 2000 for toy-related injuries. Since 1978, the U.S. Consumer Product Safety Commission has had to issue recalls of children's toys including animals (stuffed and unstuffed), balls, blocks, boats, cars, clocks, clowns, dolls, flashlights, guns, helicopters, jewelry, jump ropes, music boxes, musical instruments, nursing bottles, planes, play sets, play houses, rocking chairs, stacking rings, tea sets, telephones, trains, trucks, wagons, water slides, and whistles. In October and November 2000 alone, the National Association of State Public Interest Research Groups found thirty-four potentially hazardous toys on store shelves. Toys provided to children in doctors' waiting rooms, pediatric wards, and intensive care units can harbor dangerous strains of bacteria. Children exposed to soft plastic toys could absorb phthalates, chemicals that have been linked to kidney damage, are probable carcinogens, and may cause reproductive abnormalities. Now let's see you try and explain all this to your three-year-old when he's whining for the latest cool plastic robot advertised on TV.

## TRAFFIC (see also BOSTON, CHICAGO, LOS ANGELES, MIAMI, PHOENIX, PORTLAND, SAN DIEGO, SAN FRANCISCO, SEATTLE, WASHINGTON)
Congestion in sixty-eight urban areas of the U.S. during 1999 cost $78 billion and caused commuters 4.5 billion hours of delays, an increase in the average annual traffic delay per person from eleven hours in 1982 to thirty-six hours in 1999. And there are still people out there claiming that they drive because it's quicker than walking.

## TRAINERS, AIR CELLS IN

Basketball players are four times as likely to twist their ankles if they wear trainers with air cells in the heels. This could be because they get distracted by the thought of how much they paid for the things.

---

### TRAMPOLINES
#### (see also SPORTS)

What goes boing, boing, boing, *ouch?* Trampoline injuries—including sprains and fractures that are often severe and can result in paralysis or death—lead to medical, legal, insurance, and disability costs, and other expenses of nearly $300 million annually.

---

## TRAUMA

We assume you didn't think trauma was good for you to begin with, but it's even less fun than you thought. Experiencing traumatic events such as child abuse, an auto accident, combat, rape, a school shooting, or an earthquake can result in post-traumatic stress disorder, a condition involving changes in brain chemistry that can last a lifetime and produce hypervigilance, anxiety, fearfulness, nightmares, or emotional numbness.

## TRAVEL (see also AIRPLANE TRAVEL)

In case our wonderful world tour hasn't got the message across yet, here it is: *stay home.* One traveler in thirty requires emergency care while abroad. In addition, travelers are subject to gastrointestinal disorders and may acquire diseases such as malaria, hepatitis A and B, typhoid, amebiasis, polio, and meningitis, as well as tuberculosis and rabies. Women traveling outside the U.S., Canada, and Europe during pregnancy have a heightened risk of acute toxoplasmosis.

### TREES (see also FLOWERS, GRASS, WEEDS)
Allergies can be caused by trees including oak, elm, birch, ash, hickory, poplar, sycamore, maple, cypress, walnut, and western red cedar. Reagan did his best to stamp out this menace to society, but the little suckers are still out there.

### TRUCK DRIVER, BEING A (and see WORK)
Truck drivers are at unusually high risk of contracting bladder cancer. Drinking coffee reduces the risk of bladder cancer (see COFFEE, NOT DRINKING). Truck drivers drink lots of coffee. None of this makes sense to us, either.

### TRUCKS (see also TRAFFIC)
One diesel truck can produce as much pollution as one hundred cars, pouring substances into the air that can lead to asthma, lung cancer, and global warming; and more than one million trucks on the road today do not meet current pollution standards (as defined by the Official EPA Dictionary: "As long as your vehicle can be seen from a distance of three feet, you're not emitting too much smoke").

### TRUMPETS
Amateur trumpet players may have a heightened risk of strokes. Their neighbors may have a heightened risk of STRESS.

### TUNA BURGERS (see also FOOD)
Tuna burgers can cause histamine poisoning. Still, when was the last time you ate a tuna burger?

**danger** warning
**caution** warning
**danger** warning

**u**

## TUNISIA (see also AMERICA, CHINA, DOMINICAN REPUBLIC, EGYPT, INDIA, KENYA, MEXICO, PERU)

And now, for those of you who are still grimly hanging on by the skin of your immune systems, the last stop on our worrying world tour: Tunisia! In that heartening study, more than 30 percent of the tourists who traveled to Tunisia got sick. Next year, just go to Oklahoma or somewhere (though not NORMAN).

## TURKEY (see also FOOD)

Think twice before you give thanks for your turkey. The Center for Science in the Public Interest has documented more than twenty-one outbreaks of food poisoning linked to turkey between 1990 and 1997. One turkey in six tested by CSPI was contaminated by campylobacter, the leading bacterial cause of food-borne diarrhea.

## ULTRASOUND

Ultrasound scans during pregnancy can result in babies being LEFT-HANDED. Big deal; the real question is, if it can flip their brain hemispheres, what *else* is it doing in there?

## UNMARRIED, BEING (see also MARRIAGE)

People who are unmarried have worse diets, more mental problems, lower incomes, and a tendency to die earlier (no wonder they're not married). If you're unmarried, you're more likely to be late in seeking treatment for melanomas and cervical cancer, making your prospects for successful treatment less likely. Widowed and divorced men have high rates of suicide. Unmarried men have higher levels of heart disease than married men. If you have a good accountant, you can probably claim your wedding costs as tax-deductible health expenses.

## VALENTINE'S DAY (see also HOLIDAYS)

A study in the U.K. found that Valentine's Day can cause feelings of insecurity and depression both in single people and in those in relationships. We're not sure who has a better reason to get depressed: the singles sitting at home eating those candy hearts that taste like chalk, or couples trying to look delighted with the two-foot-square 'Love is...' cards they gave each other.

## VEGETABLE OIL (see also FOOD)

Partially hydrogenated vegetable oil, especially if consumed in sweetened baked goods, oils, and condiments, might cause colorectal neoplasia and adenomas (whatever they are). Next time you buy cookies, take them home and hydrogenate them the rest of the way.

## VEGETARIAN, BEING (see FOOD, VEGETARIAN)

## VETERINARIAN, BEING A (and see WORK)

A study in the U.K. found that suicide is three times more common among veterinarians than in the general population. Well, if you spend much of your time with your hand inside a cow, any alternative is going to look good.

## VETERINARY CLINICS

Outbreaks of salmonella have been reported among employees and clients of veterinary clinics. (We thought you only got salmonella from eating contaminated food; what *is* the vet doing with your poodle in there?)

## VIDEO GAMES (see also COMPUTER GAMES, MOVIES, TELEVISION)

Sure, they keep the kids quiet for a few hours—but not in the long run. Playing video games is likely to be even worse than watching violent movies and television programs in terms of creating aggressive attitudes, values, and behavior, especially in children, as well as desensitizing people toward violence in real life.

### VIRUSES (see also DISEASES)
Some human viruses of the sort that cause colds, diarrhea, or pinkeye may also result in obesity. Oddly, though, nobody claims you can cure pinkeye with exercise and willpower.

### VITAMIN A, TOO LITTLE

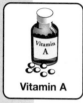
Vitamin A

And now, our special Vitamin Catch-22 supplement! Let's take a look at what happens to you if you take too much, or too little, of your favorite vitamins (and honestly, what are the odds you're taking the right amount?). To start from the beginning, vitamin A deficiency may lead to cervical neoplasia in women infected with HIV.

### VITAMIN A, TOO MUCH
On the other hand, too much beta carotene, which is used as a vitamin A supplement, can increase the risk of cancer, especially for smokers. (If you quit SMOKING, of course, you wouldn't have to worry about this.) High doses of vitamin A can also injure the liver and—in older women—increase the risk of hip fractures.

### VITAMIN C, TOO LITTLE
Confused yet? Check this out: taking too little vitamin C can increase the risk of high blood pressure, strokes, cardiovascular mortality, age-associated cognitive decline, and cancer.

### VITAMIN C, TOO MUCH
But taking too much vitamin C can cause diarrhea, kidney stones, oxidative damage to DNA in cells, and hardening of the arteries. Pick your problem!

## VITAMIN D, TOO LITTLE

Don't worry (well, yes, worry), there's more. Taking too little vitamin D can increase the risk of breast cancer.

## VITAMIN D, TOO MUCH

But don't push it: vitamin D builds up in the body and, if taken in overdoses over long periods, can lead to bone or muscle pain, constipation, diarrhea, drowsiness, headache, loss of appetite, nausea or vomiting, and more severe conditions including birth defects, high blood pressure, and death.

## VITAMIN E, TOO LITTLE

Isn't this fun? Taking too little vitamin E can increase the risk of high blood pressure, coronary artery disease, strokes, reduced cognitive function, and (when the vitamin would be taken in the form of gamma-tocopherols, whatever they may be) prostate cancer.

## VITAMIN E, TOO MUCH

Taking too much vitamin E can cause hemorrhaging or strokes. There's only one solution: put all your vitamins into one big bowl, take a handful at random whenever it occurs to you, and see what happens.

### VITAMINS (see also VITAMINS A, C, D, E)

Older people who take multivitamin supplements may get less benefit from influenza shots. Weren't the darn things supposed to be *good* for us?

### WALKERS, BABY (see also BABY CARE)

Keep the kid at home in bed (continued): during 1999, more than 9,300 children under the age of five were injured in the United States in accidents involving baby walkers, primarily as a result of falling down stairs.

## WASHINGTON, D.C. (and see CITIES, TRAFFIC)

Basically, if you live in Washington, put this book down and start packing *now,* while you still can. Washington has the highest murder rate in the U.S., more than three times the average for major American cities, and the highest murder rate among world capitals, more than twenty times the average for cities like London and Paris. Washington also ranks first among U.S. cities in cancer deaths, second in people dying of pollution from power plants, and third in terms of the percentage of travel taking place in congested traffic conditions. And we have no evidence on this one, but living so close to all those politicians (or *being* one of all those politicians) cannot be good for anybody.

## WATER (see also DRINKS)

No matter what else is full of hidden dangers, at least drinking eight glasses of water a day is good for you, right? Hahahahaha. At least one study suggests that the more tap water women drink while pregnant, the more likely they are to have spontaneous abortions. Even water that meets the minimum standards of the Environmental Protection Agency may contain disinfection by-products that are associated with bladder cancers, disease-causing micro-organisms that cause gastrointestinal illnesses in children and the elderly, lead and arsenic, and Cryptosporidium parasites that can kill people with weakened immune systems (which makes you wonder what, exactly, would *not* meet the standards of the EPA). Antibiotics and other drugs have also been found in drinking water.

## WATER, BOTTLED

Bottled water may be no healthier than tap water, costs up to a thousand times as much, is subject to less strict safety standards, and contributes to climate change through the toxic chemicals released during the manufacture and disposal of bottles. Plus, carrying those little bottles around announces to the world that you have way too much disposable income for your own good.

## WEALTH (see also POVERTY)
If you've got a history of mental illness, start giving your money away (our address is available through the publisher): rich people with this kind of history are more likely to commit suicide than poor ones.

## WEAPONS, LETHAL (see GUNS)

## WEAPONS, NON-LETHAL
From the Official Los Angeles Police Dictionary: "non-lethal, adj. Might not kill you if you duck fast enough." Between 1996 and 2000, sixty-nine people were hit by so-called "non-lethal" "bean-bag" rounds fired from shotguns by police in Los Angeles. Forty-four of those hit suffered serious injuries, and one man died.

## WEB, THE (see INTERNET)

## WEEDS (see also FLOWERS, GRASS, TREES)
Allergic reactions can be caused by weeds such as ragweed, sagebrush, pigweed, Russian thistle, and cocklebur. Learn to live with it: weedkiller can do a lot worse.

## WEIGHT-LOSS PRODUCTS (see also EPHEDRA, HERBAL REMEDIES)
Weight-loss products may contain ephedra, an herb that can raise blood pressure and cause reactions such as vomiting, heart palpitations, dizziness, nervousness, and even heart attacks, seizures, and strokes. On the other hand, being even a

few pounds overweight means you come in for the kind of treatment that can cause most of the same symptoms. Your call.

## WELDER, BEING A (and see WORK)

Being a welder may lead to contracting Parkinson's disease. That can't be a good combination.

---

### WEST, THE

**(see also EAST, MIDWEST, SOUTH; and see NEVADA)**

Looks like a lot of people out in the Wild West still think they're Billy the Kid: the West is the region of the U.S. with the highest rate of crimes against person and property. The future doesn't look good, either: global warming will stress migrating fish in the region, damage desert ecosystems, and reduce peak runoff from mountain areas, complicating water management for flood control, cities, and irrigation.

---

## WEST VIRGINIA (and see STATES)

West Virginia is the fourth most unhealthy state in the U.S. Are you sure you want those country roads to take you home?

## WINTER (see also SUN, TOO LITTLE; and see SPRING, SUMMER, AUTUMN)

Don't get all carried away with spring fever and start making babies: being born in late winter has been linked to schizophrenia and affective psychosis later in life. And that New Year's Eve clinch isn't a good idea either: children conceived in the winter are more likely to develop a common childhood brain cancer called medulloblastoma.

## WOMAN, BEING A (see also MAN, BEING A)

We were all pretty sure that being a woman in this society couldn't be good for you; and here's the evidence. Women have twice as many mood disorders during their lifetimes as men (and if we all think hard and compare our paychecks, our rape risks, our promotion statistics, and the comments we get as we pass building sites, we can probably figure out a few of the reasons). Women are also more likely to suffer from some diseases (notably autoimmune diseases such as multiple sclerosis, rheumatoid arthritis, and myasthenia gravis) and to react adversely to others: compared with men, for example, women with coronary artery disease have significantly lower levels of mental well-being three years after being diagnosed. Women who have heart attacks arrive later at the hospital and are less likely than men to receive appropriate treatment, leading to worse long-term outcomes. And women are less able than men to find their way in unfamiliar places. (They get there faster anyway, though, because they ask directions.)

## WORK (see also COLLEAGUES, OFFICES, SHIFT WORK, STRESS; and see AIRLINE CABIN CREW, ARTIST, BARBER, CARPENTER, CARPET LAYER, CHEMICAL MANUFACTURING, CONSTRUCTION, CRUSHING AND GRINDING, DAY CARE, DENTIST, DOCTOR, DRY CLEANER, EMBALMER, FARMING, FURNITURE, GARBAGE COLLECTOR, HAIRDRESSER, HOTEL CLERK, JANITOR, LIBRARIAN, MECHANIC, MINER, MUNITIONS PLANT, MUSICIAN, NURSE, NURSING HOME, PAINTER, PRIEST, PRINTER, PROSTITUTE, PSYCHIATRIST, PUBLIC RELATIONS, REFEREE, RESPIRATORY THERAPIST, SAND, TAXI DRIVER, TEXTILE, TRUCK DRIVER, VETERINARIAN, WELDER, WRITER)

If you're looking for a way to sue your employer (and who isn't?) have we got news for you! Problems at work can be blamed for mood and sleep disturbances, upset stomachs, headaches, cardiovascular disease, musculoskeletal problems, psychological disorders, disruptions in your relationships with family and friends, and susceptibility to diseases such as colorectal cancer. Tell your boss to start being very, very nice to you.

## WORK, NOT HAVING
Surprise, surprise: people don't go on welfare for the good of their health. Being unemployed is strongly correlated with depression, anxiety, poor health, and high death rates.

## WORKING HOURS, LONG
If you live at the office and can't remember what your house looks like in daylight, don't be too pleased with yourself. Compared with men who work seven to nine hours a day, men who work more than eleven hours have double the risk of heart attacks.

## WORKING HOURS, SHORT
On the other hand, you don't need to envy your independently wealthy cousin who checks in at his office twice a week and can't remember his job description, either. Compared with men who work seven to nine hours a day, men who work less than seven hours have triple the risk of heart attacks.

## WORKPLACES (see ANTIQUE STORES, BOWLING ALLEYS, DRY CLEANERS, FLOWER SHOPS, GAS STATIONS, LIQUOR STORES, NURSING HOMES, OFFICES, SHIFT WORK, THRIFT STORES)
Don't think you can get around this one by working from home (see HOMES).

## WRESTLING (see also SPORTS)
And after all that effort they put into being beautiful: wrestlers are particularly susceptible to boils.

## WRINKLES, NOT HAVING

People with fewer wrinkles in their faces run a greater risk of basal cell carcinoma. You might want to think twice about that face-lift.

## WRITER, BEING A (and see WORK)

When you're coming to the end of a book, take a moment to think about the dangers someone faced to bring you that work of art. Writers have an unusually high risk of dying from pulmonary tuberculosis.

## ZOOS, PETTING

Farm animals in petting zoos may transmit E. coli bacteria, which can be dangerous, especially for young children. Introduce your kids to Animal Planet instead. (This week: The Planet's Funniest Bacteria! Emergency Vets Go to the Emergency Room! And coming soon, our new series: Children Who Run with the Germs!)

## ZZZZS (see SLEEP)

# sources

I did not make any of this up (except the various Official Dictionaries, which don't exist but should, and the large man with the Henry Ford T-shirt). All the information in this book comes from the sources whose websites are listed on pg. 139–43.

Having spent countless hours prowling these sites, though, I advise a certain caution in taking at face value what they say (and therefore what I say). Even the most respectable sources can draw sweeping conclusions from limited or ambiguous information, get the facts wrong, imply incorrectly that one thing causes another just because both happen at the same time, be contradicted by other stories, leave out vital background material, rely on research or comment by parties with a financial interest in what's being reported, or simply reflect bias on the part of writers or editors. And even if the stories are "right," they may be superseded by later findings that overturn what everyone thought they knew.

When it comes to pinning down things that are bad (or good) for you, reality can be elusive. If you have reason for concern about any of the entries in these pages, you should probably investigate further before panicking. (This doesn't count entries like SMOKING—if you smoke, panic now.) A good place to start is the Internet, which is an endless source of information and surprises. Simply go to a search engine like Google (www.google.com), enter the issue you're concerned about, and prepare to scroll through 862,417 relevant Web pages.

News accounts and helpful links can be found by searching the websites of *USA Today* (www.usatoday.com), the BBC (www.news. bbc.co.uk), the *New York Times* (www.nytimes.com), the *Guardian* (www.guardianunlimited.co.uk), and CNN (www.cnn.com). For links to more technical material, try *Medscape* (www.medscape.com), *Newswise* (www.newswise.com), *Science News Online* (www.sciencenews.org), or *InteliHealth* (www.intelihealth.com). Useful magazines and journals include *Scientific American* (www.sciam.com), the *Journal of the American Medical Association* (http://jama.ama-assn.org), and the *British Medical Journal* (www.bmj.com).

Government agencies are a basic source of information; see, for example, the Centers for Disease Control and Prevention (www.cdc.gov), the Consumer Product Safety Commission (www.cpsc.gov), or the Medline Plus feature of the National Institutes of Health (www.nlm.nih.gov/medlineplus). Independent organizations with useful points of view include the Center for Science in the Public Interest (www.cspinet.org), and Public Interest Research Groups (www.pirg.com).

Don't believe everything you read, though.

# websites

Agence Française de Sécurité Sanitaire des Aliments
  <www.afssa.fr>
AirSafe Journal <www.airsafe.com>
American Academy of Allergy, Asthma and Immunology
  <www.aaaai.org>
American Academy of Family Physicians, "American Family
  Physician" <www.aafp.org>
American Academy of Neurology <www.aan.com>
American Academy of Orthopaedic Surgeons
  <www.arthroscopy.com>
American Academy of Pediatrics, "Pediatrics" <www.aap.org>
American Academy of Sleep Medicine <www.aasmnet.org>
American Association of Neurological Surgeons
  <www.neurosurgery.org>
American Board of Family Practice, "Journal" <www.abfp.org>
American Cancer Society <www.cancer.org>
American Foundation for Suicide Prevention, "Lifesavers"
  <www.afsp.org>
American Heart Association <www.americanheart.org>
American Lung Association <www.lungusa.org>
American Medical Association, "Archives of Family Medicine"
  <http://archfami.ama-assn.org>
American Medical Association, "Archives of Pediatrics and
  Adolescent Medicine" <http://archpedi.ama-assn.org>
American Medical Association, "Journal of the American
  Medical Association" <http://jama.ama-assn.org>
American Orthopaedic Society for Sports Medicine, "The
  American Journal of Sports Medicine" <www.sportsmed.org>

American Psychiatric Association, "American Journal of Psychiatry" <http://ajp.psychiatryonline.org>

American Psychological Association <www.apa.org>

American Society for Microbiology <www.asm.org>

American Veterinary Medical Association, "Journal" <www.avma.org>

APB Online <www.apbnews.com>

Associated Press <www.ap.org>

British Association of Urological Surgeons, the European Society of Paediatric Urology and the Societé Internationale d'Urologie, "BJU International" <www.blackwell-science.com>

British Broadcasting Company News <news.bbc.co.uk>

"British Medical Journal" <www.bmj.com>

Cable News Network <www.cnn.com>

Center for Science in the Public Interest <www.cspinet.org>

Center for Science in the Public Interest, "Nutrition Action Healthletter" <www.cspinet.org/nah/>

Clear the Air <www.cleartheair.org>

"Crime Times" <www.crime-times.org>

Discovery Health <www.health.discovery.com>

Explore St. Louis <www.explorestlouis.com>

Friends of the Earth <www.foe.org>

"Globe and Mail" (Toronto) <www.globeandmail.com>

Greenpeace <www.greenpeace.org>

"Guardian" Unlimited (UK) <www.guardianunlimited.co.uk>

Harvard University Kennedy School of Government <www.ksg.harvard.edu>

Harvard University Medical School, "Harvard Health Letter" <www.health.harvard.edu/newsletters/hltext.html>

Information Ventures, Inc. <www.infoventures.com>

InteliHealth <www.intelihealth.com>

International Society for Environmental Epidemiology,

"Epidemiology" <www.epidem.com>
Internet Mental Health <www.mentalhealth.com>
"Irish Independent" <www.independent.ie>
"Irish Times" <www.ireland.com>
Ivanhoe Broadcast News <www.ivanhoe.com>
Josephson Institute of Ethics <www.josephsoninstitute.org>
"Journal of Epidemiology and Community Health"
  <www.jech.com>
"Lancet Interactive" <www.thelancet.com>
Mayo Clinic Health Oasis <www.mayohealth.org>
Medscape <www.medscape.com>
"Men's Fitness" <www.mensfitness.com>
"Men's Health" <www.menshealth.com>
Mental Health Foundation (U.K.) <www.mentalhealth.org.uk>
"Merck Manual of Diagnosis and Therapy" <www.merck.com>
"Military Medicine"
  <www.amsus.org/militarymedicine/milmed.htm>
"Mothering: The Magazine of Natural Family Living"
  <www.mothering.com>
National Institute of Mental Health, "Schizophrenia Bulletin"
  <www.nimh.nih.gov/researchfunding/schizbull_2005.cfm>
National Sleep Foundation <www.sleepfoundation.org>
National Women's Health Information Center
  <www.4woman.gov>
"Nature Science Update" <www.nature.com/nsu>
"New England Journal of Medicine" <www.nejm.org>
"New Internationalist" <www.newint.org>
"New Scientist" <www.newscientist.com>
"New York Review of Books" <www.nybooks.com>
"New York Times" <www.nytimes.com>
"New Yorker" <www.newyorker.com>
Newswise <www.newswise.com>
Norman Convention & Visitors Bureau <www.ncvb.org>

ParentCenter.com <www.parentcenter.com>

Pneumotox On Line <www.pneumotox.com>

Public Citizen <www.citizen.org>

Public Interest Research Groups <www.pirg.com>

Reuters Medical News via <www.medscape.com>

Samaritans (UK) <www.samaritans.org>

"San Francisco Chronicle" <www.sfchron.com>

"Science News Online" <www.sciencenews.org>

"Scientific American" <www.sciam.com>

"Sunday Times" (UK) <www.timesonline.co.uk>

Texas Transportation Institute <http://tti.tamu.edu>

"Time" Magazine <www.time.com/time>

"Times" (UK) <www.timesonline.co.uk>

U.N. Development Program <www.undp.org>

U.N. Environment Program <www.unep.org>

U.N. International Labor Organization <www.ilo.org>

U.N. World Health Organization <www.who.int/en/>

Union of Concerned Scientists <www.ucsusa.org>

U.S. Census Bureau <www.census.gov>

U.S. Centers for Disease Control and Prevention
   <www.cdc.gov>

U.S. Centers for Disease Control and Prevention,
   "Morbidity and Mortality Weekly Report"
   <www.cdc.gov/mmwr/>

U.S. Consumer Product Safety Commission <www.cpsc.gov>

U.S. Department of Health and Human Services
   <www.hhs.gov>

U.S. Department of Justice, Bureau of Justice Statistics
   <www.ojp.usdoj.gov/bjs>

U.S. Department of Justice, National Institute of Justice
   <www.ojp.usdoj.gov/nij>

U.S. Department of Labor <www.dol.gov>

U.S. Food and Drug Administration <www.fda.gov>

U.S. General Accounting Office <www.gao.gov>

U.S. Global Change Research Program <www.usgcrp.gov>

U.S. National Cancer Institute <www.nci.nih.gov>

U.S. National Institute of Allergy and Infectious Diseases
<www.niaid.nih.gov>

U.S. National Institute of Arthritis and Musculoskeletal and Skin
Diseases <www.nih.gov/niams>

U.S. National Institute of Diabetes & Digestive & Kidney
Diseases <www.niddk.nih.gov>

U.S. National Institute of Environmental Health Sciences,
National Institutes of Health <www.niehs.nih.gov>

U.S. National Institute of Neurological Disorders and Stroke
<www.ninds.nih.gov>

U.S. National Institute for Occupational Safety and Health
<www.cdc.gov/niosh/homepage.html>

U.S. National Library of Medicine, "Medline Plus"
<www.nlm.nih.gov/medlineplus>

U.S. National Library of Medicine, "PubMed"
<www.nlm.nih.gov>

U.S. Occupational Safety & Health Administration
<www.osha.gov>

U.S. State Department <www.state.gov>

"U.S.A. Today" <www.usatoday.com>

"Washington Post" <www.washingtonpost.com>

Web Guide <www.webguide.com>

Web MD <www.webmd.com>

World Bank <www.worldbank.org>

World Book's Fun & Learning <www.worldbook.com>

World Conservation Union <www.iucn.org>

World Resources Institute <www.wri.org>

World Wildlife Fund <www.worldwildlife.org>

WWF-UK <www.wwf-uk.org>

Yahoo! News <www.yahoo.com>

# about the author

David French has held jobs ranging from disc jockey and school bus driver to university professor. He also worked for many years with agencies trying to assist economic development in poor countries. He has had the opportunity to observe things that are very bad for you while living in places like Nigeria (during a civil war), Eritrea (whose government expelled him from the country), Malawi (home of the world's most dangerous snakes), Italy (home of Italian drivers), and Angola (another civil war). He has written about these and other experiences in publications such as the *New York Times Magazine*, *Commonweal*, *World Development*, and *The Natural Resources Forum*, and he has published a book on communal workplaces. He currently lives in Dublin, Ireland, where he is trying to develop a more positive frame of mind through the study of Buddhism.